BEYOND BUZZWORDS

BEYOND BUZZWORDS

Why Some Ideas Fail to Improve Instruction

Robert L. Jorczak

ROWMAN & LITTLEFIELD
Lanham • Boulder • New York • London

Published by Rowman & Littlefield
A wholly owned subsidiary of The Rowman & Littlefield Publishing Group, Inc.
4501 Forbes Boulevard, Suite 200, Lanham, Maryland 20706
www.rowman.com

Unit A, Whitacre Mews, 26-34 Stannary Street, London SE11 4AB

Copyright © 2017 by Robert L. Jorczak

All rights reserved. No part of this book may be reproduced in any form or by any electronic or mechanical means, including information storage and retrieval systems, without written permission from the publisher, except by a reviewer who may quote passages in a review.

British Library Cataloguing in Publication Information Available

Library of Congress Cataloging-in-Publication Data

Names: Jorczak, Robert L., author.
Title: Beyond buzzwords : why some ideas fail to improve instruction / Robert L. Jorczak.
Description: Lanham, Maryland : Rowman & Littlefield, 2017. | Includes bibliographical references and index.
Identifiers: LCCN 2017000648 (print) | LCCN 2017010200 (ebook) | ISBN 9781475834758 (cloth : alk. paper) | ISBN 9781475834765 (pbk. : alk. paper) | ISBN 9781475834772 (electronic)
Subjects: LCSH: Effective teaching. | Teaching—Methodology. | Education—Aims and objectives.
Classification: LCC LB1025.3 .J676 2017 (print) | LCC LB1025.3 (ebook) | DDC 371.102—dc23
LC record available at https://lccn.loc.gov/2017000648

Printed in the United States of America

CONTENTS

Preface vii
Introduction xi

1 The Goals of Improved Instruction 1
2 What Evidence? 11
3 Big Ideas, Little Evidence 21
4 What Can Improve Instruction? 35
5 An Information Processing Instructional Model 55
6 Instructional Support for Internalization 65
7 Supporting Externalization 81
8 Instructional Environments 97
9 Peer-to-Peer Collaborative Learning Methods 105
10 Using the I-E Instructional Model to Design High-Quality Instruction 115

Bibliography 131
Index 133
About the Author 137

PREFACE

This book is intended to help all instructors improve their instruction. K–12 teachers, higher-education instructors, trainers, and instructional designers can all benefit from the evidence-based instructional model presented in this book. That model aligns instruction with established theory of how students learn. The model can make clear what is ineffective or inefficient with your current instruction and indicate how to improve.

Educational researchers and practitioners are influenced by several popular ideas that are evident in most media reports about education, practically every published educational research report, and presentations at educational conferences. These ideas are said to result in either greatly improved student learning or in equity of opportunity to learn. Because such ideas tend to be both easy to understand and oft repeated, they achieve a status that is not commensurate with supporting scientific evidence or alignment with scientific learning theory. The ideas have become *buzzwords* that guide instructional thinking and practice; they gain the focus of educational policy but lack sufficient evidence of improving instruction or student learning.

Buzzwords that are in vogue tend to change over time, though some have exhibited staying power. All instructors are familiar with a number of such buzzwords that are found in school mission statements, teacher preparation texts, and instructional self-help books. This book intends to identify some educational buzzwords, explain whether they make sense theoretically, and evaluate supporting evidence (or lack thereof).

This book does not, however, merely attack popular concepts that lack sufficient evidence. The information presented in this book moves beyond critique of buzzwords to provide a deeper understanding of why some instructional methods can be expected to work better than others. Instructional topics are examined and explained from an evidence-based theoretical perspective. This perspective provides a basis for critically evaluating educational methods, programs, and products that are touted as solutions to educational problems or said to provide huge improvements in instructional effectiveness.

Beyond Buzzwords presents instructional alternatives that have theoretical and empirical support. In addition to presenting a coherent model of instruction, the book also addresses key concepts relevant to instruction in the early twenty-first century, such as differences between online and classroom instructional environments and benefits of peer collaboration for learning.

BASIS

Evidence-based instruction is instruction founded on principles with sufficient evidence obtained from scientifically valid research. The foundational principle guiding this book is that scientifically derived principles of how humans learn provide the best basis for understanding how to improve instruction. This may seem obvious, but some recommendations encountered in educational research and literature fail to meet this criterion. What exactly the phrase "evidence-based" means must be better understood to determine whether an educational idea actually has valid supporting evidence.

Not being scientists, instructors cannot be expected to sort through and evaluate the scientific validity of educational research. This book therefore seeks to interpret scientific learning research expressed with common instructional concepts and terminology understood by instructors. In other words, this book seeks to be a bridge between *scientifically valid* learning research and instructional practice.

The model of instruction presented in this book, along with the many evidence-based instructional principles included, remove the burden of educators having to seek evidence for every proposed instructional idea or method. Instead, following the instructional model will ensure evidence-based practice and indicate which new instructional ideas have a good chance of succeeding.

In addition to scientific evidence, effective instructional guidance has been provided by best practices within the instructional profession. Indeed, practice-based advice is based on many years of teacher experience and often agrees with evidence-based instructional theory. Best practices, however, can lack the foundation of empirical evidence and coherence provided by principles derived from scientific theory. Recommendations from practice are more susceptible to easy answers and ideological wishful thinking that promotes adoption of popular buzzwords to guide instruction.

WHAT THIS BOOK IS NOT ABOUT

This book does not address many aspects of being a better teacher. It is important to recognize that the profession of teaching involves much more than instruction. Teaching requires many diverse demands and tasks, including managing the behaviors of groups of students, assigning grades, dealing with social and personal issues of students, dealing with parents, and so on. Instruction is only one, albeit important, task of teachers.

An excellent instructor who lacks other professional teaching skills will likely fail. On the other hand, instruction is a very important teaching task and one over which teachers exert much control. Teachers cannot succeed if they are poor instructors, and likely all teachers can benefit from instructional improvement.

Beyond Buzzwords is not a research report and does not seek to present evidence of instructional effectiveness as in formal research reviews. As this book seeks to be of practical use to instructors, formal presentation of research results and evidence is beyond its scope. Some references to reports and articles are included for those seeking more information.

This book differs from many how-to-teach books in that it does not provide recipes or step-by-step instructions for instructional design (though a later chapter does provide steps for getting started in creating an evidence-based design). Knowledge about how students learn and the principles linking choices of instruction to effective or efficient achievement is expected to provide a flexible foundation within which teachers can determine the details of implementation.

The focus of *Beyond Buzzwords* is generalizable principles, not specific procedures, though some specific procedures are discussed. Thus, this book seeks to promote improved instructional practice by providing deeper understanding about why instruction works instead of providing a rote list of steps to be followed to achieve a design.

Beyond Buzzwords is not a list of alternative instructional methods nor is it an analysis of frequently used methods. Instead I seek to help instructors understand what matters for evaluating instructional methods. The details of how to implement principles are mainly left to the instructor, who is likely more familiar with target students, target outcomes, available resources, and the delivery environment of his or her situation. Understanding why some choices are better than others enables instructors to more generally apply their knowledge rather than simply following a procedure.

Buzzwords may lack evidence or may be too vague to be useful, but some contain a grain of truth. To improve instruction, however, one must move beyond buzzwords to understand the evidence-based principles involved in learning and instruction. This book seeks to clarify such principles with an eye toward improving instruction.

INTRODUCTION

What instructors generally do, by simply following best practices within the profession, is instructionally effective. Decades of instructional practice have led to reasonably effective instructional methods that are commonly used in schools. The goal of this book is to improve instruction, not revolutionize education.

If teachers are doing reasonably well at instruction, why write a book about how to improve instruction? One reason is that identifying how instruction should work will make instruction both more effective and more efficient. Instructors may be wasting effort and time on practices that lack evidence of effectiveness.

Another reason is that education has a long history of "revolutions" that failed to deliver. Many popular ideas said to improve student learning either are too vague or lack evidence and so result in less efficient or effective instruction. The history of instructional guidance includes a seemingly endless list of recommendations and concepts that are purported to radically improve instruction but do not. One sure sign of a buzzword is a promise of huge improvements in student learning or revolution of education in general. Science tends to support incremental improvements rather than radical change.

Beyond Buzzwords begins at the beginning by examining the goals of instruction. Chapter 1 examines instructional goals, including overall goals of formal education and targeted student learning goals such as those found in state learning standards (or the Common Core curriculum). Chapter 1 also provides evidence for expectations about what *can* be accomplished by improving instruction. Such reasonable goals may surprise many instructors and educators.

Chapter 2 addresses the nature of evidence. Criteria for being evidence-based are presented, and types of educational research are discussed. The chapter explains some of the difficulties and limitations of educational research. The chapter explains why much educational research deemed evidence-based is really not based on strong or even valid evidence.

Chapter 3 identifies some popular and strongly promoted instructional ideas that lack clarity or sufficient evidence (i.e., buzzwords). Some popular ideas and ideologically driven practices have little evidence of improving instruction. Popular and ideologically appealing ideas have resulted in misconceptions among instructors about how educational theory can support real-world instruction. This book seeks to dispel some popular misconceptions about instruction by enabling instructors to better determine the potential merit of new instructional ideas and products.

Chapter 4 introduces basic concepts of learning and instruction used throughout the book, especially the concept of a learning theory. The chapter describes *information processing learning theory*, which is the basis of the instructional models and principles presented in later chapters. A fuller understanding of that basis will better enable instructors to apply an evidence-based instructional model in various instructional situations.

Chapter 5 defines an instructional model and presents a model based on information processing learning theory. The model guides better instructional practice and provides a means to evaluate proposed instructional methods said to improve instructional quality.

Subsequent chapters discuss aspects and elements of the instructional model in more detail, especially focusing on principles that guide instructional actions. Later chapters address aspects of instruction associated with instructional environments (i.e., classroom versus online) and the popular collaborative learning method.

Each chapter includes "externalizations" in the form of questions for reflection or discussion by the reader. Writing out answers to some of the questions will improve your learning of the information in this book and your understanding of the presented instructional model. Discussing the questions with others is also beneficial.

INTRODUCTION   xiii

SOME QUESTIONS WITH ANSWERS

1. What is evidence-based instruction and why does it matter?

Evidence-based instruction uses instructional strategies and methods that are supported by valid and ample scientific research. Scientifically valid instruction can be expected to provide the most effective instruction just as scientifically valid medical practice provides the best chance to improve health issues. These days, however, almost all educational programs, products, and methods are said to be evidence-based. Critical analysis is required to determine if evidence from research is sufficiently valid scientifically. Aspects of instructional principles and interventions being evidence-based are discussed in chapter 2.

2. Is evidence-based instruction, or following the instructional model presented in this book, a shortcut to school improvement?

To answer this question, exactly what "school improvement" means must be clarified. The model presented in this book is purported to improve instruction in terms of effectiveness and efficiency, which is only part of what schools are about. The presented model is a shortcut in that understanding the model can help instructors improve instruction more reliably and quickly than trial and error or buzzwords. What improved instruction can and cannot accomplish is a major focus of chapter 1.

3. Is there a road map I can use to ease into evidence-based practice?

This book attempts to provide such a road map, but it does not provide explicit step-by-step recipes that can lead instructors to better practice without a good understanding about why the model is expected to work.

4. If you know how to do evidence-based instruction, will you enhance your future position to retain your job?

If you are an instructor, the answer is likely yes. Educational institutions such as the U.S. Department of Education and local school districts increasingly promote evidence-based instructional practice. School boards and administrators are increasingly looking for instructors to justify their methods as evidence-based. The trend is so prevalent that "evidence-based" is in danger of becoming a buzzword (see chapter 2). Understanding what evidence-based really means, and being able to defend your instruction as following an evidence-based model, positions you to justify your instruction as evidence-based.

5. *Is there an executive summary for policy makers and administrators that provides the gist of benefits of evidence-based instruction without reading the whole book?*

You do not have to read the book from beginning to end to understand and use the presented instruction model. Chapter 5 introduces the model that simply asserts that instruction requires support for two distinct learning processes: internalization and externalization of information. Different cognitive processes and instructional variables are involved in optimizing instructional support for each learning process.

Chapters 6 and 7 review how those variables affect instructional quality in some detail. The principles in those chapters can guide better instruction. Educators and administrators who do not instruct will likely benefit more from the early chapters that address expectations of improving instruction, critical evaluation of evidence, and a review of questionable but popular instructional concepts and methods.

6. *Are there dos and don'ts for getting started with evidence-based instruction? Are there myths that might derail efforts?*

The biggest myth that could derail efforts to improve instruction is that educational theory and research cannot effectively inform instructional practice. It can. In fact, it is the best basis for informing instructional practice. No simple list of dos and don'ts can guide instructors to better practice without an understanding of the concepts of better instruction.

7. *How should I read this book?*

With a relaxed and open mind. Several complicated topics are addressed though effort is made to use terms and concepts familiar to all instructors. Feel free to take it slow and think about the concepts presented. Allow yourself time to process the information presented. Skip about if you like. Take what you need or what you are interested in.

1

THE GOALS OF IMPROVED INSTRUCTION

What this chapter is about: This chapter examines what instruction is trying to achieve and also what improved instruction means.
Why that matters: The first step in achieving goals is clarifying them. Also, such analysis can specify what can be achieved and what cannot.

A goal of instruction often stated by educational policy makers is to promote achievement of targeted learning outcomes (objectives, standards, etc.) by all students for each grade level. The targeted outcomes for this goal tend to be minimum competency standards. The idea is to give all students some minimum level of knowledge that enables them to succeed in life.

Other goals are possible. For example, instruction could seek to have each student learn as much as they can within an instructional period. This latter goal seeks to optimize the learning of each student rather than ensure that all students meet a set of learning outcomes. Instruction supporting this goal would be very different than instruction intended to get all students "over the bar" of minimum competency.

The first goal implies that *improved* instruction will increase the number of students that achieve targeted learning outcomes compared to unimproved instruction. But this definition leaves open the question about how much instruction can be improved (i.e., how many more students can achieve the outcome) or how much effort and expense is involved in getting more students to achieve target outcomes.

Intuition and hope lead us to believe that improving instruction can significantly increase the number of students who achieve targeted outcomes. Evidence, however, should be the basis for deciding if and how much improved instruction can help us meet educational goals. What exactly improved instruction can achieve is a question that is best answered by examining evidence.

Unfortunately, surprisingly little attention is paid to the evidence. The idea that instruction can make all learners learn what we want them to learn is ideologically and politically desirable, so we tend to assume it is true.

Intuition also leads us to believe that improved instruction can help us achieve any educational goal. For example, many people assume that improved instruction can overcome large disadvantages of students underprivileged by our society or that instruction can eliminate differences in time students need to learn. Instruction is assumed by some to have unlimited ability to correct any ills of a society. We must, however, critically analyze evidence of what can be achieved to have the best chance of optimizing instruction in the real world.

Instructors promote learning by arranging factors (variables) of the learning environment in ways thought to improve student learning of targeted outcomes. It follows logically that improved instruction *better* arranges learning variables so that more students achieve targeted learning outcomes. Scientific evidence should be able to indicate how many more achievers to expect from improved instruction. Without such evidence, we have no scientific basis to have any expectations about improving instruction.

HOW MUCH CAN INSTRUCTION IMPROVE LEARNING?

We have plenty of sound evidence that instruction works. Students who receive instruction perform better than those who do not. What often is not addressed is how much the quality of instruction matters. In other words, how much can improved instruction reduce the time it takes students to achieve learning goals or increase how many more students achieve goals in a fixed time? Little thought is given to limitations of what improved instruction can and cannot accomplish or the cost and effort required to accomplish specific improvements.

THE GOALS OF IMPROVED INSTRUCTION

Unfortunately, the specifics of a principle relating instructional quality to student learning are not yet known. What can be said is that improving instruction likely has diminishing returns after some level of instructional quality is achieved. After a threshold of quality is achieved, little improvement in the number of students who achieve target learning will be realized by further improving instruction.

EXPECTATIONS FOR INSTRUCTIONAL IMPROVEMENT

Educational researchers have ample evidence that differences in students account for much of the variation in student learning performance. Students vary greatly in learning ability, prior knowledge, self-regulation, and motivation. All these variables strongly affect learning speed. Evidence indicates that such student differences matter much more for learning performance than do differences in the instruction they receive. Even optimized instruction cannot completely compensate for differences in students and get all students to learn at the same speed.

The landmark Coleman Report in the 1960s examined more than three thousand schools for various factors thought to affect student learning. The factors associated with 90 percent of the variation in student learning performance included student aptitude and family socioeconomic status (SES)—factors of students beyond the control of the school or educational system. Only the remaining 10 percent of student performance difference was associated with differences in school quality factors, *including teachers and instruction*.

A report by Schochet and Chiang (2010) employs modern hierarchical statistical analysis to summarize research of factors affecting formal learning. The average correlation (across many studies) of school differences on the variation in student performance is 0.01, and the correlation of different classrooms (i.e., teachers) within schools is 0.03. A much higher correlation of 0.92 was found for student variables that are not under the control of a teacher.

Instructors cannot realistically be expected to get all of a group of diverse students to meet learning objectives in a fixed time period. Factors within students that cannot be set or changed by instruction are too powerful in determining student performance in comparison to the effect of instruction. Even if instruction is optimized to the student, instruction cannot ensure that all students learn at the same speed.

In classrooms, instruction is typically *not* optimized to individual students—all tend to get the same instruction despite their different characteristics. Given group-based instruction and a limited time frame, instructors must make a choice they would rather avoid. For which students should instruction be optimized? Should instruction target a mythical typical student in the class, or should the instruction focus on struggling students?

Instruction likely cannot be optimized for both groups. Optimizing for the majority will likely result in nonoptimal instruction for struggling students. Choosing to focus on the struggling students may well result in less-than-optimized instruction for most students in the class. In either case, instruction will not maximize learning for students with greater ability, more prior knowledge, and high motivation. The realities of classroom environments mean that teaching a group of students in a limited time frame will likely result in some students not achieving the learning objectives, *regardless of instructional quality*.

One proposed solution is for the instructor to "differentiate" instruction for subgroups of students with similar learning characteristics or to individualize instruction for every student. Differentiated instruction, however, increases the instructional burden on instructors, which is likely to decrease quality. Completely individualized instruction is beyond the capabilities of classroom instructors without additional resources unavailable in typical classrooms. Educational costs are certain to greatly increase if every student receives individualized instruction.

Research evidence that indicates that improved instruction cannot level the playing field so that all students learn equally quickly is very disappointing to educators and instructors. Instruction, however, cannot change reality to align with our ideology or wishes, no matter how noble the goals of that ideology. As practical instruction in a real-world educational system involves many limitations, we must accept limitations on what real-world instruction can accomplish.

The achievable goal for improved instructional quality is to increase the number of students achieving goals or reduce the time required by most students to achieve learning outcomes. Just how much differences in instruction can improve learning performance is an open question. Instruction, however, is one of the few things instructors can control to improve learning. Thus, improving instruction to the point of optimal effectiveness is well worth the effort despite the fact that it cannot solve all educational problems or get all students to learn equally.

GOALS OTHER THAN ACHIEVING LEARNING OUTCOMES

Many people have high expectations that improving instruction can solve various societal and educational problems. Some politicians and parents believe that improved instruction can solve issues stemming from cultural attitudes or inequities of our society. Educational goals beyond increasing the number of students who achieve targeted learning outcomes, however, likely cannot be achieved by improving instruction because the factors causing these problems are outside of educational control. The subtle effect of improved instruction likely cannot compensate for the effect of equity differences of society.

For example, the current (and long-standing) goal of eliminating the racial and ethnic achievement gap is probably not achievable by improved or differentiated instruction. Differentiated instruction to eliminate ethnic differences implies that some types of instruction work better for one ethnic or racial group than other groups, an idea not supported by evidence.

Expectations of improving learning by improving instruction must be based on an analysis of what can possibly be achieved. Such analysis must also include an estimate of the potential effect of improving instruction compared to improving other factors that affect learning.

The limitations of what can be accomplished via instruction are offered not to discourage or excuse instructors for poor results, but rather to use research evidence to establish realistic goals for real-world instructional environments. Expecting instruction alone to compensate for all educational and social problems is unreasonable. Optimizing student learning within the limitations of the instructional environment is a sufficient goal for instruction.

LEARNING OUTCOMES

The immediate and obvious goal of instruction is achievement of target learning outcomes. State learning standards are statements of what *should* be learned. The science of learning and instruction cannot determine *what* should be taught (i.e., learning outcomes or standards). Experts, including experienced teachers, community representatives, and subject experts, are tasked with determining what should be learned.

The focus of instruction, in contrast, is *how* to help students learn what should be learned. Different types of learning outcomes often require different types of instruction. Ideally, educational researchers should provide scientifically sound principles that prescribe effective instruction for different types of outcomes. Classifying learning outcomes, therefore, is the place to start when designing and optimizing instruction.

Opinions vary among researchers about how to classify types of learning outcomes. Various classification schemes (taxonomies) have been offered. Many educators are familiar with Benjamin Bloom's taxonomy of learning. Bloom provides six cognitive outcome categories that are the focus of formal education: knowledge, comprehension, application, synthesis, analysis, and evaluation.

Anderson and Krathwohl (2001) revised Bloom's categories by transforming the category labels from nouns to verbs: remember, understand, apply, create, analyze, and evaluate; thereby changing Bloom's categories from types of knowledge to behaviors or tasks. Anderson and colleagues further define four *types* of knowledge: factual, conceptual, procedural, and metacognitive. This change reflects the idea that learning outcomes have two dimensions: type of knowledge but also knowledge *use*.

Table 1.1 is a learning outcome taxonomy that includes knowledge types and uses that are supported by research into how students learn. Rote knowledge is like a recording; the only use possible is to play the recording back (i.e., recite the knowledge). Concepts and principles can be used in various ways. A student can state a principle, or they can solve a specific problem using the principle. This taxonomy will be revisited in more detail in a later chapter. The point here is that a learning taxonomy is useful in defining instructional goals (learning outcomes).

INSTRUCTION FOR DIFFERENT TYPES OF OUTCOMES

Evidence indicates that specific instructional methods are more effective for achieving specific kinds of objectives. For example, rote learning and learning facts require rehearsal (in other words, repetitive processing) such as with drill and practice. Many concepts are effectively taught by presenting examples and nonexamples and having students classify examples while providing feedback. Generative outcomes, which require students to create new knowledge, are difficult to achieve via instruction because they involve cognitive skills in addition to knowledge.

Being able to state a concept is an example of knowledge *use* (i.e., stating). Recalling and stating a principle is very different from being able to apply the concept (by, for example, classifying items as examples of the concept or not). Therefore, taxonomies of learning outcomes should include the two dimensions of knowledge—type and use (e.g., the rows and columns of table 1.1)—that are the basis of selection of effective instructional methods.

CONCEPTUAL CHANGE

Changing students' current knowledge (conceptual change) via instruction is much more difficult than adding new knowledge. The nature of

Table 1.1. Taxonomy of Learning Outcomes for Two Dimensions

Use/Type	Recall	Use Specifically	Use Generally	Discover/Generate
Rote	recite	N/A	N/A	N/A
Facts	state	answer question	N/A	find
Concepts	state	classify	classify generally	create
Principles	state	predict	predict generally	infer
Procedures	state	accomplish task	apply to other tasks	find

how knowledge is stored (discussed in more detail in a later chapter) maintains students' existing knowledge and also works to reestablish old knowledge.

Information that contradicts students' existing knowledge is discomforting. The most common student response is to simply ignore conflicting information (and no conceptual change occurs). Alternatively, students can alter the new information to somehow conform to what they already know and perceive it as a slight modification to what they already know. Lastly, they can change their belief, fully achieving targeted learning.

Conceptual change requires much more instructional effort than simply adding new elements to students' prior knowledge. Conceptual change may require a different type of instruction that accounts for students' current beliefs. Learning-outcome goals become much more difficult to achieve via instruction when students already have misconceptions about the outcomes.

INSTRUCTIONAL GOALS SUMMARY

While the clear goal of instruction is to help as many students as possible achieve targeted learning outcomes, people often expect that instruction can guarantee that all students will achieve all targeted learning. When the limitations of real students in real learning environments are considered in light of learning research, higher-quality instruction cannot guarantee that all students will learn targeted outcomes in typical learning environments that limit instructional time. Instruction cannot have as its goal the curing of societal ills that instruction does not affect.

Nevertheless, education is so important that we owe it to our students and our society to provide the best instruction possible. The good news is that sufficiently specifying learning outcomes enables better prescription for how to teach for those outcomes, and therefore learning outcomes specified in terms of knowledge type and use are essential for improving instruction and increasing student achievement of learning goals.

QUESTIONS

How would you answer the following questions? It would be better for learning to write your answers and edit them until you are totally satisfied with your answer. You also should think about what questions you would ask about instructional goals.

1. What is your goal in respect to learning outcomes when you instruct students? Do you seek to get as many students as possible to achieve targeted learning outcomes, or do you seek to lessen the time to learn of every student?
2. How many more of your students would have to achieve targeted outcomes to justify improving your instruction?
3. What goals do you have for your instruction beyond helping students achieve specified learning outcomes? Why do you believe instruction can help achieve those goals?
4. How does having different goals affect instruction? For example, how does teaching a concept differ from teaching a procedure?
5. What different instructional methods are appropriate for the five different types of knowledge listed in table 1.1? Do you think different instructional methods are optimal for the four different uses of knowledge?

REFERENCES

Anderson, Lorin W., and David R. Krathwohl. *A Taxonomy for Learning, Teaching, and Assessing: A Revision of Bloom's Taxonomy of Educational Objectives*. New York: Longman, 2001.

Schochet, Peter Z., and Hanley S. Chiang. "Error Rates in Measuring Teacher and School Performance Based on Student Test Score Gains" (NCEE 2010–4004). Washington, DC: National Center for Education Evaluation and Regional Assistance, Institute of Educational Sciences, U.S. Department of Education (2010).

2

WHAT EVIDENCE?

What this chapter is about: This chapter explains what evidence-based really means and indicates what makes evidence stronger.
Why that matters: Empirical evidence is the scientific basis for knowing what instructional actions can result in higher-quality instruction.

A major premise of this book is that evidence-based research should guide educational practice. Many instructional interventions (methods and products) claim to be evidence-based or research-based. What makes an educational intervention evidence-based, however, is not clear. This chapter focuses on issues of determining the validity and strength of research evidence that should be the basis of being labeled evidence-based.

Empirical evidence results from repeatable testing of hypotheses, which are tentative statements of prospective principles. Evidence from research either supports or denies proposed hypotheses. Hypotheses with evidence are accepted as principles that are true or, more correctly in a scientific sense, less wrong than other principles. Supporting tests differ in quantity and quality that define the strength of the evidence. The quantity of evidence depends on the number of different studies done to test a principle. Research quality is determined by study design and execution.

Evaluating the strength of evidence is difficult because educational research is complicated and has uncertain results. Limitations of educational research, such as ethical limits of research on humans and practical limits of research in schools, make ideal educational research hard to achieve. Many variables can affect educational research results, but they are difficult to control. Determining exactly which variables are responsible for observed results is often equivocal.

For technical reasons, research in actual educational settings often cannot establish *causal* relations between variables of instruction and student learning. Most educational research looks for relationships in data but cannot establish what is causing the observed relation. Coincidence (mere chance) or some unknown variable could be causing the relation.

Much published educational research, even in peer-reviewed journals, does not meet the criteria of valid scientific research. Even less research is valid for universal educational application. Many findings apply only to specific situations. Educational research is complicated, so investigation into how instruction can be improved is difficult and hard to interpret.

Because good educational research is difficult to achieve, it is important to evaluate supporting research claims as weak or strong, including peer-reviewed published research. Because of the many technical factors involved in educational research, educators and instructors may not be able to effectively evaluate research evidence. Instructors should adopt a position of caution about claims of support from evidence.

Educators should ask questions about research offered as supportive of instructional principles and products. Does the evidence come from a single study or a single group of researchers? Is the evidence from an experiment? Are compared groups equivalent in terms of instruction or type of students? Answers to such questions can help instructors evaluate the strength of claims of being evidence-based.

RESEARCH QUANTITY AND REPETITION

The difficulty of educational research means that no single study, or small set of studies, can "prove" a principle or the effectiveness of an instructional intervention. Evidence obtained from many studies is stronger than evidence from a few studies or a single study. Studies must be replicated (i.e., repeated) to increase the credibility and applicability of the findings. Several studies from diverse researchers are required to have confidence that a principle or method is evidence-based.

Research studies related to theories with much supporting evidence are stronger than those without theoretical support. A valid scientific theory is based on much diverse evidence that lends support to principles of the theory. Stronger theories display consilience with theories and evidence from other fields of study, increasing the amount of support. For example, evidence of learning principles from educational studies that agree with evidence from neuroscience and medicine is stronger than principles from educational research only.

Quantity, however, is no guarantee of scientific validity. Research also differs in quality of the research design, how well the researchers executed the design, and how well the researchers analyze and interpret the results. Much poor-quality research is not as valid as less high-quality research.

RESEARCH METHODS AND QUALITY

Research can be classified based on the type of research method used. Study methods can be experimental, quasi-experimental, or descriptive (aka correlational or observational). All these method types should employ measurement and statistical analysis (i.e., use quantitative methods). Qualitative research makes no measurements and is focused on collecting and categorizing information. Qualitative research is generally not sufficient for a claim of being evidence-based, but such research could support a "research-based" label.

Educational research often seeks to establish whether (and how much) a difference in an input variable (such as instructional intervention type) affects differences in an outcome variable (such as student learning). Research is seeking evidence about a principle—how much changes in variable A affect variable Z. Studies of instruction tend to test whether intervention A affects outcome Z (often student learning) more or less than intervention B (or no intervention).

Experiments (also called randomized controlled trials or RCTs) support *causal* conclusions—that changing variable A caused result Z. For example, that using a new instructional method results in less time for students to learn a specific outcome. Experiments also require that students be randomly assigned to the compared groups.

In an ideal experiment, researchers change the value of a variable (e.g., A) for two comparison groups while keeping all other variables fixed and equal between the groups. All other variables are controlled (held constant or evenly distributed between the groups). The researchers then measure any changes in an outcome variable of interest (e.g., Z), such as student learning, to see if the groups perform differently. Any difference can only be due to the difference in A because all other variables did not change. The change in A must have caused the difference in the outcome variable.

Experiments in the real world are not ideal, and compromises are often made that damage the strength of the evidence of the experiment. Much can go wrong. Not all variables can be controlled. Experiments may lack sufficient numbers of students for random assignment to equalize variables in each group. Study results can be flawed or simply wrong because the studies are poorly designed (e.g., lack sufficient control of variables). All experiments are not of equal quality. A poor experiment provides weaker evidence than one that is better designed and executed.

Quasi-experiments are studies in which a variable is intentionally made different for two (or more) groups, but the researchers do not randomly assign students to the groups. The researchers cannot be sure the groups are equivalent for all other variables. Researchers cannot be sure that the change in the controlled variable caused any observed changes in the outcome variable because the groups may not be equivalent for other variables.

Quasi-experiments are quite common in education because students are placed into classes by schools. Classes are convenient groups. In many "real-world" studies, researchers compare the result of a difference, for example, a different instructional method, on two different existing classes. As students are not randomly assigned to classes (in most cases), researchers cannot be sure that other differences in the groups did not cause observed changes in learning between the classes.

Other study methods are labeled observational/descriptive/correlational. With this type of study, researchers do not control variables or group assignment and therefore cannot conclude what caused any observed difference in the measured outcome variable. Data are analyzed

Table 2.1. Types of Research Studies

Type of Study	Defining Characteristics	Strengths	Weakness
Experiment	1) Manipulation of input variable. 2) Random assignment of students to groups.	Can support casual inferences.	Difficult to do. Rare in educational research.
Quasi-experiment	1) Manipulation of input variable. 2) Students are not randomly assigned to groups.	Practical in school settings with classes. Comparison in an authentic context.	Does not support causal inferences. Common in educational research.
Descriptive/Observational Studies	1) No variables manipulated. 2) Students not assigned to groups. 3) Correlations (relations) in data are simply noted.	Easy to do. Do not require disruption of the instructional process.	No causal inferences. Observed correlations may be due to chance.

for relations among variables, but researchers do not implement a procedure that might affect students. Descriptive research methods can provide evidence, but that evidence is very tentative. Such studies are ambiguous about cause and so the evidence is not nearly as strong as experiments.

For example, a descriptive study might ask how the sex of the student is related to learning algebra. Researchers can neither control the sex of a student nor assign students to one of the sexes. Differences may be observed, but the cause of the differences in learning algebra cannot be unequivocally attributed to students' sex.

Some evaluators of educational research reserve the label "evidence-based" only for studies that are experiments. Unfortunately, much educational research does not use experiments. The difficulty of implementing high-quality experimental designs in actual educational environments results in many descriptive studies.

A review of 144 federal contracts for evaluation studies from 1995 to 1997 by Boruch, DeMoya, and Snyder (2002) found only five experiments. A survey of published research of technology education by Johnson and Daugherty (2008) found no randomized control experiments in a survey of 199 studies. While the number of educational research experiments is increasing, these findings should lead to caution in conclusions about supportive evidence in education.

Even experimental research can fail to be of high quality for various reasons such as use of an invalid comparison group. The results of some experiments apply only to the very specific situations of the study. The findings may not hold true for other situations. The Institute of Education Sciences (IES), which evaluates educational research and sets quality guidelines, finds that most educational research falls well short of even minimum quality standards.

EVIDENCE-BASED AS A BUZZWORD

The term "evidence-based" is increasingly found in education books and government policy documents. U.S. government research funding agencies and school districts now insist that all instructional interventions be evidence-based. However, the definition of evidence-based has increasingly been weakened so that the term has become meaningless.

The U.S. Department of Education (DOE; 2016), based on the Every Student Succeeds Act (ESSA), has issued guidance for labeling the strength of studies based solely on the study type:

> The term "evidence-based," when used with respect to a State, local educational agency, or school activity, means an activity, strategy, or intervention that . . . demonstrates a statistically significant effect on improving student outcomes or other *relevant outcomes* based on—
> (I) *strong evidence* from at least one well-designed and well-implemented experimental study;
> (II) *moderate evidence* from at least one well-designed and well-implemented *quasi-experimental study*; or
> (III) *promising evidence* from at least one well-designed and well-implemented correlational study with statistical controls for selection bias.

Additionally, the U.S. DOE recommendation allows the evidence-based label for research studies that "demonstrate a rationale" based on research findings. This definition of evidence-based intervention allows almost any intervention with a published educational study to be labeled "evidence-based." This guideline basically turns the term "evidence-based" into a buzzword that can be applied to any intervention subjected to any type of study. The U.S. DOE simply applies a modifier of "strong," "moderate," or "promising" to the evidence-based label.

The claim that "evidence-based" can be a buzzword might seem odd in a book that promotes evidence-based instruction. However, simplistic and unrealistic definitions of what evidence-based means have led to uncritical application of the label to nearly every new instructional intervention.

As with all buzzwords, people have sought easy answers that lack depth of understanding. Educators (and the U.S. DOE) prefer experiments or quasi-experiments in classrooms that pit very specific interventions (often instructional products) against (often undefined) comparison interventions. Such research, however, lacks sufficient control of variables to say *why* the intervention works. Also, results cannot be generalized to other instructional environments, situations, and students. So, even when an experiment supports an assertion, educators would do well to ask whether their situation is similar enough to the tested situation.

New interventions are often compared to alternatives described as "traditional" or "business as usual," which does not specify exactly to what a new intervention is being compared. Being evidence-based should imply that an intervention is designed based on empirically established theory and principles, but, in fact, the new intervention merely showed evidence of superior results compared to an unspecified method, product, or curriculum.

The suggestion that we can improve instruction by comparing interventions and simply using the one with the observed better performance is an illusion. A more useful focus is on theory and research that identifies widely applicable principles rather than comparisons of the relative performance of two very specific intervention products that differ in materials, student and instructor motivation, instructional time, and other learning variables.

META ANALYSIS EVIDENCE

An alternative to intervention-comparison studies being labeled evidence-based involves results from *meta analyses* (research that aggregates results from many studies). Such research summaries usually measure differences as *mean effect sizes* across many studies that investigate an intervention. Mean effect sizes are metrics of average differences that allow comparisons of the effects of diverse interventions. For example, one could compare the effect size of eating junk food prior to instruction to the effect of whether or not instruction includes feedback.

Calculating mean effect sizes of an intervention across many studies provides stronger evidence of an effect than a single study. But interpreting the strength of evidence requires a good understanding of the caveats and limitations of the meta analytic process.

Results from meta analyses are often used to compare the relative effects of very different interventions. Some educational writers have published lists of mean effect sizes to establish that some interventions are more effective than others. Meta analyses resulting in effect size comparisons have some value, but such comparisons are dangerous because they often compare apples to oranges in ways that are not valid.

For example, a list of effect sizes might show that instruction with "feedback" has twice the effect of "mastery learning." The problem with such comparisons is that mastery learning may or may not include feedback. Different types of feedback (and mastery learning) are possible, and we cannot be sure that the simplest form has little effect.

Unfortunately, mean effect size comparison has become an easy way to make large claims about instruction in educational literature and in the minds of many instructors. The caveats of those who understand the limitations of meta analysis are largely ignored. Instructional recommendations based on results from many statistically merged comparisons of diverse interventions require careful interpretation. Understanding what meta analysis can really tell us, and the limitations involved with interpreting such results, is difficult and best left to experts instead of serving as easy guides to higher-quality instruction.

SUMMARY

The goal of this chapter is primarily to make instructors aware of the difficulty of critically evaluating claims of various instructional recommendations, principles, and products as evidence-based. The complexities of valid scientific research for effective instructional practice make evaluating claims very difficult. A useful rule-of-thumb is to be skeptical and pay more attention to the amount and kind of evidence supporting a claim. An alternative is to rely on well-supported principles from established theory in evaluating an intervention rather than results from a few studies.

Because instruction is complicated and because it so important for the success of our children, instructors must be dubious of easy answers, vague general concepts, panaceas, and beliefs based on ideology of what we want to believe as opposed to reality.

QUESTIONS

1. Think of an educational idea or recommendation that you believe in and use regularly. What evidence supports that idea (be specific)? Do many experimental studies underlie your beliefs?
2. Think of an instructional intervention (a method, curriculum, or product) that has recently been suggested to you or your colleagues that was described as evidence-based. How much research evidence did those supporting the product reference? (Look it up if you can.) Were the referenced studies experiments, pseudo experiments, or descriptive studies?
3. What sort of evidence would convince you that the recommendation for a new intervention that is contrary to what you have been doing works as claimed?

REFERENCES

Boruch, Robert, Dorothy DeMoya, and Brooke Snyder. "The Importance of Randomized Field Trials in Education and Related Areas." In *Evidence Matters: Randomized Trials in Education Research*, edited by F. Mosteller and R. Boruch, 50–79. Washington, DC: Brookings Institution Press, 2002.

Johnson, Scott D., and Jenny Daugherty. "Quality and Characteristics of Recent Research in Technology Education." *Journal of Technology Education* 20.1 (2008): 16–31.

U.S. Department of Education. *Non-regulatory Guidance: Using Evidence to Strengthen Educational Investments*. Washington, DC: Department of Education, 2016.

3

BIG IDEAS, LITTLE EVIDENCE

What this chapter is about: This chapter reviews popular ideas about how to improve instruction that lack sufficient clarity or evidence (i.e., buzzwords).

Why that matters: Popular reformist ideas that lack evidence of improving instruction distract instructors from changes that can increase instructional quality.

Many people, including media pundits, assert the idea that the U.S. educational system is broken or somehow deeply underperforming. Over many years, people have promoted educational "reform" as a means to compensate for the perceived effects of a failed school system. This chronic belief that our educational system is deeply flawed and responsible for many of our social problems has led to many educational movements and efforts to implement changes in the educational system.

Unfortunately, the theoretical support and empirical evidence underlying reform ideas do not match the fervor of reformers. Supporting evidence for most of the reform ideas is either missing entirely or is presented without scientific critical analysis. Historically, the drive to reform often is based on intuition and ideology rather than evidence.

The history of instructional reform is rife with ideas offered as solutions to educational problems that failed to deliver significant improvement. Popular instructional ideas have been accepted as greatly improving instruction without sufficient evidence to justify the high expectations. Most have mostly failed to make significant changes in overall student performance.

For example, the shock of the supposedly technologically backward Soviet Union launching the first artificial satellite in 1957 led to a reform movement that stressed increased science and math instruction and made such instruction more hands on (students were led to do science rather than just learn scientific facts). Sound familiar? Such concern about the performance of U.S. math and science students is still common more than fifty years later, despite changes in instruction.

Current efforts to reform math and science instruction include attracting more women and minorities to science, technology, engineering, and math (STEM) and stressing a hands-on activity-based instruction (e.g., discovery learning). Advocates seem unaware that their recommendations have already been tried and ultimately did not fix the perceived problem. As is often the case, a noble goal is sufficient to sustain the movement with little consideration about the evidence of effectiveness.

Major changes and even revolutions in education have been repeatedly proposed, but very few improvements and revolutions have occurred. The failure of concepts and principles with little valid evidence to deliver instructional improvement often leads instructors and educators to doubt the value of evidence-based research.

Reformers assert this lack of result is due to the entrenched conservatism of educational institutions and unwillingness of schools to change. Or the failure of reform is attributed to the opposition of groups such as teacher unions or behaviorists. Actually, the characteristics of U.S. student learning performance are determined less by the education system and more by U.S. culture. For example, U.S. popular culture promotes the idea that people good at math lack social skills, which makes math learning unappealing. U.S. culture finds it acceptable for people to say, "I suck at math" without the embarrassment they might feel if they said, "I suck at reading." Failings of U.S. society are reflected in the U.S. educational system, not caused by it.

The variables reformers identify as causing or affecting learning often are unclearly defined. Principles involving general and ill-defined constructs are prone to being seen as panaceas, with large benefits in all instructional situations. Vague definitions, however, simply allow researchers to more easily claim that observed benefits are due to the poorly defined variables instead of the actual causes.

Another potential reason for belief in unsupported instructional interventions is researcher or educator bias. The results of limited and specific studies are interpreted based on what the researcher or educator prefers to believe. Some educational researchers misinterpret research findings to better match their ideology. When educational policy makers have a similar bias, the proposed idea becomes entrenched and small numbers of research studies are asserted as providing strong evidence, fueling a reform movement.

Educational reformers and educators tend to look for quick and easy evidence. They seek comparisons of new methods and products to older ones for "proof" that the new method works better. This sort of evidence, which holds sway over educational change, is misleading. Such single-case studies, executed poorly in very specific contexts not under the control of researchers, cannot provide the strength of evidence we need to improve education. Instead, educational decisions should be based on sound learning theory that is supported by much diverse evidence from the lab and classroom.

Examples of recent reform movements include merit pay for teachers, elimination of tenure, and increased choice for parents (via charter schools and vouchers). No scientific studies support these ideas, and in fact, several studies show that these ideas have no effect on student performance. These ideas appeal to political ideology or simple intuition about what might affect formal learning rather than strong theory-based evidence.

The money spent on these ideas far exceeds what is justified by evidence. New York City spent more than fifty million dollars on merit pay for teachers that had no effect on student performance. Millions from public school tax revenue is now paid to charter schools outside the traditional public school system, but charter school students' performance is basically identical to traditional public school students.

For various reasons (see chapter 2), many parents but also educational writers, policy makers, and administrators lack sufficient knowledge to assess the evidence related to educational proposals. People tend to rely instead on what is getting a buzz within the education community. Such reliance on what is in vogue is dangerous and leads to misconceptions. Several concepts currently commonly encountered in educational literature and in discussions among teachers lack specificity and evidence.

LEARNING STYLES

The popularity of *learning styles* among educators is an example of how misconceptions can "go viral" within the education community if they are easy to understand and match our ideology. A very popular instructional principle is that students vary in learning "style" and therefore need to be taught differently based on that style.

Learning style is a very vague and general concept. Many styles have been suggested based on various student differences. Perhaps the most popular style is based on the sensory mode employed during instruction: visual, auditory, or kinesthetic (VAK). Despite the ubiquity of this idea, variation in learning based on instructional sensory mode lacks supporting evidence. In fact, the evidence suggests against learning styles of any type (e.g., see Pashler et al. 2009).

Despite a lack of supporting evidence, many instructors have been inculcated with the idea that learning style is an important variable. Why has this happened despite weak supporting evidence? One reason is that the idea aligns with the intuitive view that all students learn differently. That view appeals because instructors recognize that specific instructional methods do not always work for all students. Students differ on many variables that affect learning, so it seems logical that students differ in how they learn.

All humans, however, have similar cognitive systems that evolved over millions of years. Human cognitive systems are more similar than different even if the knowledge in the system is quite different. Consider an analogy with walking. Surely differences in how humans walk can be identified, but the basic structure and mechanism of two-legged walking are the same for almost all walkers. So too does human learning follow a set of basic principles that apply to all human learners. Such principles are the basis for designing effective instruction, with some consideration for how learners differ.

Students certainly differ in ways that may affect how they learn and how they are optimally taught. These student variables are discussed in more detail in later chapters. How differences in student variables should affect instruction is an important part of any instructional model and should result in principles for dealing with student differences.

We have basically no evidence, however, that many of the variables suggested as learning styles can be used to improve learning. Learning different types of information can be improved by using appropriate sensory modes during instruction. In some cases, a picture is worth a thousand words. But this principle does not change for individual students. Samantha does not learn faster or better than Shawna because specific information is presented by images rather than via sounds.

The failure of utility of learning styles does not, however, negate benefits of individualizing instruction to suit the learner. Some student differences matter very much for instructional effectiveness. For example, students differ in their prior knowledge. Optimal instruction must adapt based on such differences. The learning styles concept simply focuses on differences in students (e.g., preference for sensory modes) that do not affect learning and so cannot be used to effectively individualize instruction.

ACTIVE LEARNING

Exactly what active learning means varies in educational research literature. Active learning is suggested as an important variable of instruction, but exactly what is varied is unclear. Though examples of active learning often include physical activity, mere physical activity is not what is advocated—mental activity is implied.

A common definition of active learning (which is often linked to student "engagement") is effortful student attention to, and mental participation in, instructional methods. Students, however, can be mentally active when they attend a lecture, which advocates of active learning see as passive.

Another definition adopted by instructors is that active learning includes learning activities or "learning by doing." Formal instruction, however, has always included learning activities (e.g., homework, drills, and projects). Most instructors include activities as a regular aspect of their instructional design. Only very poor and ineffective instructors simply lecture to their students.

The efficacy of learning activities is supported by strong evidence. The instructional model offered in this book explicitly recognizes the importance of learning activities for instruction. The problem with active learning is that it is too vague and general to indicate how to improve the effectiveness of learning activities or what to do for students who are uninterested in actively learning.

People learn quite well from simply hearing, seeing, or reading (i.e., by sensing of new information). Learners do not need to be physically or even consciously active to learn. People can learn from simply observing another person (observational learning). Most learning occurs via internalization of information without any other activity from learners. Moreover, some internalization is necessary for productive learning activity to occur, so some "non-active" learning is a prerequisite for active learning.

The learning model presented in later chapters of this book accepts the efficacy of having students do activities. Seeing active learning as the basis of better learning, however, misses the point about how to appropriately include student activity in an instructional design because the active learning concept is ill defined.

Some active learning proponents assert that active learning results from a *conscious effort* to learn (e.g., Richard Mayer's *active learning principle*). We know that people can learn without conscious effort via associative and implicit learning, so this principle is better stated that students learn some types of information better if they apply conscious effort to learn. The idea that conscious intent affects how quickly and well learning occurs, however, is challenged by some research. Craik and Tulving (1975) found that learning is affected more by the nature of a task performed than the intent of the learner.

Learning activities, as we shall see, are key instructional tools required for improved instruction. The popular concept of active learning, however, is a vague and simplistic concept that basically advocates against instructor lecturing without a strong theoretical basis for doing so. To be useful, active learning requires more detail about learning variables associated with having students do learning activities or pay more attention to instruction.

TWENTY-FIRST-CENTURY LEARNING OUTCOMES

Currently, a very popular assertion is that essential educational outcomes of this century are qualitatively different than previous centuries. Proponents of this idea assert that this change should be reflected in changes in instruction. Advocates of twenty-first-century skills see a greater need for social competence and collaboration skills, such as the skills advocated by proponents of collaborative and social-emotional learning (SEL).

It is easy to accept that educational content has changed. Students no longer need to be taught information for obsolete technology, jobs, or institutions. Advocates of twenty-first-century learning, however, assert not only that content has changed but that aspects of the new century require students to be taught higher-order learning outcomes (e.g., problem solving and critical thinking) and cooperative social skills.

The basis for the new needs is not clear. All centuries have needed more and better critical thinkers. Good and creative thinking has also always been needed. Social skills have always been important to humans. Some suggest that jobs and careers of this century emphasize cognition over labor. A need, however, does not imply a solution.

Increasing overall human cognitive ability may be beyond the capability of instruction regardless of need. The fact that technology and institutions of the new century are more integrated and complex and require better cognition does not at all imply that we can teach better cognition to meet that need. Formal education in the new century likely can meet job preparation needs by teaching new content and skills rather than attempting to increase cognitive abilities.

Another issue with the twenty-first-century skills movement is the assumption that the primary or only goal of formal education is to prepare students for jobs or careers. Other centuries did not have such an exclusive focus. Educational thinkers of the past suggested other goals such as informing people so they can be better citizens and make better decisions when participating in a democracy. Others have stressed that the quality of students' lives improve when students are more knowledgeable of science, art, and history.

The biggest problem with assuming new twenty-first-century educational needs stressing higher-order outcomes is that we lack evidence-based principles linking specific instructional methods to such outcomes. We are unclear about how to more effectively teach such outcomes, or even whether instruction can improve achievement of such outcomes. Surely instruction can help students better reach their potential for better cognition. Increased knowledge has many of the same effects as improved cognition. But attempting to improve the cognitive ability of students may be akin to making them all taller via instruction.

Overall, the new century likely has a need for students to learn new skills. It is the assertion that these skills are more needed and that instruction should focus on higher-order skills that calls into question the value of this buzz concept.

CONSTRUCTIVISM

As with many instructional concepts of questionable utility, exactly what constructivism is and what it recommends is vague and varies depending on who is giving the definition. Constructivism is often said to be a learning theory, but it lacks the essential explanatory nature of scientific theories. It is really more of an instructional model based on cognitive and constructivist principles.

Constructivists often say that their foundational principle is that knowledge is constructed (i.e., uniquely generated by each student). This principle is not unique to constructivism; in fact few learning theories suggest otherwise. The ramification of this principle for instruction is that *knowledge* cannot be transferred directly from instructor to student. Few instructors and even fewer theorists believe knowledge can be directly transferred, though an important point of this book is that *information can be transferred*.

The one unique principle originally asserted by constructivists is that students learn better when they guide their own learning (i.e., without guidance from an instructor). The effect of instructor versus learner control is a recurring issue of later chapters, but the relevant point here is that no strong evidence supports this principle. In fact, much evidence suggests that students learn better with instructional guidance.

More recently, constructivists have amended the principle to say that students learn better with *less* guidance (allowing that some form of instructional guidance is required). This principle also lacks strong evidence but may apply for some learning goals in some contexts.

Several studies from the 1970s looked at the effect of types of teacher behaviors on student achievement. For example, Brophy and Good (1986) surveyed research of teacher behavior on achievement and found that greater percentages of teacher talk (including lecturing) are associated with improved achievement. Soar (1966) and Soar and Soar (1972) found that indicators of high teacher control of learning tasks also correlate positively with achievement.

Overall, constructivists seem guided by the ideology of critical theory from political science and other humanities studies. Critical theory concerns societal power structures and their effects on individuals. Constructivists apply this idea to conclude that students learn best via less instructional control.

It is easy to accept that self-motivated and self-regulated students learn better even if given less guidance. Constructivists are less clear about what to do about students who lack motivation and do not learn when left to their own guidance. Minimal guidance leaves few options for instructors to address problems that arise.

Constructivists have tended to adopt many principles and methods advocated by cognitive educational psychologists. Such principles are explained by cognitive learning theories such as the information processing learning theory discussed in later chapters. What constructivism adds to the perspective of cognitivist scientists on learning and instruction is not clear. How instructors or educators benefit from constructivism is also unclear despite its strong influence on teacher preparation programs.

Overall, constructivism has some benefit in identifying poor instructional practices, such as overreliance on telling students what we want them to know. Unfortunately, supporters of constructivism go beyond recommendations against too much lecturing and assert across-the-board learning benefits based on increased learner control. A useful instructional model should indicate conditions under which less learner control is beneficial for learning.

EDUCATIONAL TECHNOLOGY

Historically, much has been made about the potential instructional benefits of new technology. Promoters of technology have asserted potentially huge improvements in learning that would revolutionize instruction. Over the years, radio, audio recording, movies, television, computers, and other technology have been offered as boons for instruction. Despite the new capabilities of such new technology, expectations of greatly improved learning have never been met.

Given the history of hyperbole associated with educational technology, assertions that the latest technology is going to bring about huge benefits are not justified without very strong evidence. This caveat applies to the current excitement about the capabilities of digital communication, the Internet, social media, and mobile learning.

Technology has always been useful for instruction. Inventors of the blackboard and cheap pencils likely claimed that students were going to learn better if their inventions were used. There is little doubt that technology has made instruction more efficient (i.e., less expensive or easier to implement) and increased student access to information and instruction, both very good reasons to adopt new technology for instruction.

Whether new technology improved student learning compared to older technology using similar instructional methods, however, is a very different question. Richard Clark (1994) and other researchers have argued that differences in media do not differentially affect learning. The major finding of research comparing instructional technologies is "no significant difference" in student performance on learning outcomes.

Clark asserts that differences in instructional methods determine learning effectiveness, not information delivery media. When differences are found in research studies of educational technology, differences in instructional methods are also present. Such differences in method tend to obscure the true cause of research results. Researchers cannot be sure whether improvements in learning are due to different technology or different instructional methods.

Comparisons of the technology must use very similar instructional methods to validly attribute learning differences to technology differences. Results are generally negative when different technology (or a different medium) is used but similar or identical instructional methods are employed.

New educational technology *can* offer educational improvements in efficiency. Research of technology use for instruction should focus on whether newer technology enables students to achieve learning outcomes more quickly or cheaply than older technology, not whether new technology is more effective.

Technology, from printed books to social media, has historically improved student access to instruction. For example, distance learning allowed students to receive instruction they otherwise could not access. Current mobile communication provides access to information and instruction from almost any location at any time. Students can now access most course materials at any time and place. All students now have access to high-quality information. Unfortunately, they also have increased access to low-quality and incorrect information.

Computers also have value in their traditional role of data management. Learning management systems (LMSs) offer a revolution in that they potentially make individualized instruction practical. Individualization is too labor intensive for teachers to totally individualize instruction without technology support. An automated process of testing, prescribing, and delivering instruction makes practical instruction suited to each student.

In summary, the claims of the huge potential of educational technology are unjustified by theory or evidence. Technology likely cannot improve the overall learning performance of students; only higher-quality instruction (or more instructional time) can do that. Technology use alone cannot eliminate achievement gaps, make all students learn equally quickly, or improve students' social skills. Effective instruction is required.

THE VALUE AND COSTS OF VAGUE AND GENERAL CONCEPTS

Overall, each term of the preceding sections has some merit. All contain a grain of truth about learning and instruction. Misunderstanding and misuse of the terms, however, leads them to be not just unhelpful but deleterious because they provide easy, thoughtless answers that lack evidence of improving instructional quality. Concepts become buzzwords when they are vague and thoughtlessly repeated as explanatory without clear definitions and supporting evidence.

The main point of this chapter is that popularity and ubiquity of instructional ideas are no guarantee of the effectiveness of such ideas. Too many strong ideological and political forces determine which ideas get the buzz. But human intuition and ideology are poor ways to determine the effectiveness of educational interventions. Educators must adopt procedures that critically examine proposed methods before adopting such methods. Concepts such as grit, metacognition, self-regulated learning, situated learning, social-emotional learning, pre-K education, and so forth need to be carefully evaluated based on the scientific evidence rather than the excitement they generate or need.

Many popular ideas are not well supported by strong evidence that meets the criteria presented in the previous chapter. Without such support, these terms cannot be described as evidence-based and cannot point the way to improved instruction. The way forward to increased instructional quality is via sound theoretical foundation and strong evidence of effectiveness.

QUESTIONS

1. Think of an educational idea or recommendation that you have encountered that was said to improve learning. Did it? Why or why not?
2. What is your definition of active learning? What do your colleagues give as a definition? Why do you think active learning improves instruction?
3. Do you already employ active learning in your instruction? If so, how? How might you increase active learning in your instruction?
4. This chapter asserts that instructional effectiveness is related to instructional method rather than instructional media. Write down your definition of an instructional method and consider how technology might affect methods.

REFERENCES

Brophy, Jere E., and Thomas L. Good. "Teacher Behavior and Student Achievement." In *Handbook of Research on Teaching*, edited by M. C. Wittrock, 328–75. New York: Macmillan, 1986.

Clark, Richard E. "Media Will Never Influence Learning." *Educational Technology Research and Development* 42, no. 2 (1994): 21–29.

Craik, Fergus I., and Endel Tulving. "Depth of Processing and the Retention of Words in Episodic Memory." *Journal of Experimental Psychology: General* 104, no. 3 (1975): 268–94.

Pashler, Harold, Mark McDaniel, Doug Rohrer, and Robert Bjork. "Learning Styles: Concepts and Evidence." *Psychological Science in the Public Interest* 9, no. 3 (2009): 105–19.

Soar, Robert .S. *An Integrative Approach to Classroom Learning*. Philadelphia: Temple University, 1966.

Soar, Robert S., and R. M. Soar. "An Empirical Analysis of Selected Follow-Through Programs: An Example of a Process Approach to Evaluation." In *Early Childhood Education*, edited by I. J. Gordon, 229–59. Chicago: National Society for the Study of Education, 1972.

4

WHAT CAN IMPROVE INSTRUCTION?

What this chapter is about: This chapter discusses learning theory in general and the information processing learning theory specifically.

Why that matters: A learning theory indicates what variables affect learning and under what conditions and is therefore the basis of an instructional model that specifies how to achieve higher-quality instruction.

Suppose that you want to help six-year-old Johnny learn to read, help seven-year-old Martha learn to add two-digit numbers, or teach Mr. Benson to use the new copy machine. What should you do to help these people reach a level of competence more quickly? What would you do to help them learn? How should they be treated differently given the different learning goals and differences in the learners?

Improved instruction depends on knowing how people learn. How people learn is stated with *learning principles*. A *scientific principle* is a statement causally linking two or more variables (i.e., a change in the value of one variable causes the other to change in a predictable way). Scientific research of learning results in a set of learning principles that link variables of students and environments to improved learning. Variables that affect learning in predictable ways are *learning variables*.

Knowing how these variables affect learning is important in designing optimal instruction. For example, research has established a relation between learners' attention to information and their learning of the information. Increased attention (a variable) leads to better recall of the information (another variable, the outcome). Instructors try to get students to better attend to the information they present, but they must consider inherent differences in students' ability to pay attention.

SCIENTIFIC THEORIES

Scientific theories explain why some principles are true and also predict other principles. Scientists propose multiple theories to explain phenomena at the leading edge of understanding. The issue of which theory is correct is open until scientific testing can provide sufficient evidence to support one theory. The goal of scientific investigation is to determine which theory is less wrong (or to revise a theory to be less wrong).

For example, the Sun-centered model (another word for theory) explains the observed movement of planets and predicts other aspects of their motion. Ancient astronomers initially used an Earth-centered model to explain planetary movement. Copernicus suggested a heliocentric alternative. Observations and tests eventually determined that the Sun-centered model better explains the observed planetary motion. The Sun-centered model also better predicts future locations of the planets and is therefore the accepted theory of the structure of the solar system.

Two contradictory theories cannot both be correct. Two theories explaining gravity would not satisfy scientists, nor would the suggestion that both Sun- and Earth-centered systems are correct. Scientists seek to have only one theory that best explains and predicts principles. The testing of existing and newly predicted principles (i.e., empirical evidence) is the primary means used to evaluate theories. Newer theories are subject to evaluation by empirical testing (i.e., scientific basic research). Older theories have much supporting evidence and are rarely questioned unless contradictory evidence is found.

LEARNING THEORIES

Psychologists and biologists have studied how humans and other animals learn. They have identified many principles of learning and have attempted to explain those learning principles with theories. As a learning theory explains how learning occurs, it identifies ways to help people learn. Determining how to instruct or improve instruction therefore requires identification of a valid and comprehensive learning theory.

A learning theory should not be taken as valid simply because it is plausible, because it aligns with what we prefer, or because it is popular. Some theories are not testable, and some do not make predictions. Such theories are scientifically invalid.

Some theories have more supporting evidence than others. Some learning theories are more comprehensive than others in that they explain many more learning principles. A valid learning theory requires ample evidence from different sources that comprehensively predicts and explains observed learning principles. Explaining why learning occurred after the fact is not as strong as predicting the conditions under which learning will occur.

A problem with some popular learning theories is that they attempt to explain vague and hard-to-measure cognitive concepts in terms of other vague and hard-to-measure concepts. Principles of these theories are hard to test. Some theories may merely label a complex construct and treat that label as an explanation. Steven Pinker in his book *How the Mind Works* explained this labeling:

> Many explanations of behavior have an airy-fairy feel to them because they explain psychological phenomena in terms of other equally mysterious psychological phenomena. Why do people have more trouble with this task that with that one? Because the first one is "more difficult". Why do people generalize a fact about one object to another object? Because the objects are "similar". Why do people notice this event and not that one? Because the first event is "more salient". These explanations are scams. Difficulty, similarity, and salience are in the mind of the beholder, which is what we should be trying to explain. (85)

Educators should be aware that some would-be theories simply make up new variables and assert the new variables explain learning when actually the variables just label observed behavior. For example, one could assert that some students fail to learn because they have more "failureness." We can measure failureness easily by carefully amassing data about students who fail to achieve targeted learning outcomes. Despite the appearance of actual scientific research, this variable explains nothing. Failureness is a buzzword.

Psychology is a relatively new science. No current learning theory is comprehensive in explaining learning or is universally accepted. Some current learning theories tend to address proposed cognitive variables that cannot be directly observed and measured and are therefore open to the criticism of being airy-fairy labels that do not explain or predict. Many do not meet the requirement criteria of testability and comprehensiveness.

Some learning theories that address complex (and often vague) variables are constructed to explain observed principles. Theories addressing higher-level mental constructs must ultimately rely on more basic cognitive and behavioral principles to support such constructs. Higher-level constructs must operate via foundational principles of how the human brain works. Theories involving complex mental constructs may be useful, but to be scientifically valid, they must be tied to basic cognitive principles established by cognitive theory and neuroscience.

For example, the construct metacognition, often defined as thinking about one's thinking, is basically thinking and therefore subject to the basic principles of cognition. Theories about the importance of authentic practice must explain why being authentic matters for learning in terms of basic brain functions associated with learning. Without such connection to basic individual cognitive learning functions, a theory is likely merely descriptive, without adequately explaining how the construct results in improved learning.

Developmental learning theories by Jean Piaget and Lev Vygotsky are often cited in educational literature, including published research. These theories tend to describe learning in terms of constructed variables that are hard to measure (like equilibrium and cultural influence) rather than explain and predict learning based on basic cognitive processes. These theories are not well connected to the neurobiology of human nervous systems or the functions of human cognition and memory.

Vygotsky's social development theory highlights the role of interpersonal (i.e., social) interaction in human learning. Social interaction indeed seems to be very important for human learning. Humans seem "wired" to learn from other humans, especially their family, friends, teachers, and culture.

Theories of the importance of social interaction for learning ideally would explain *why* social interaction is important based on factors of individual cognition, but the theory is not explicit on such points. Modern knowledge of cognition was not available to Vygotsky, but his modern supporters have not made explicit why human learning is dependent on human interaction.

HOW DO WE KNOW WHICH LEARNING THEORY IS TRUE?

Some educational commentators assert that adopting a theory is a matter of perspective or epistemology. Deciding which theory is correct depends on the subjective philosophy of each theorist or instructor. From this perspective, the truth or value of a theory is determined by personal attitudes and choices. For example, constructivists have different views than behaviorists about conditions that contribute to learning because they have a different perspective about learning.

No doubt people tend to believe theories based on their prior knowledge and their preferences. From a scientific perspective, however, we have a means to determine which perspective better predicts and controls learning. That means is empirical evidence. Evidence can be interpreted in different ways, but if the evidence is not clear, then the principle must be further tested to distinguish which theory is less wrong. Better testing is required to resolve which theory is correct.

Some educators like the idea of multiple learning theories because they like to pick and choose among alternative theories to support their instructional preferences. This preference for multiple theories is not consistent with scientific effort to identify the least-wrong theory. Selection of theories by preference or convenience is not a good basis for educational practice.

The bottom line is that not all proposed theories are equal. They differ in the amount of supporting empirical evidence, in the number of principles they predict, and in their connection to foundational theory. To promote evidence-based instruction, educators should ask which theory results in clear principles that are supported by valid empirical evidence and are explanatory and predictive rather than merely descriptive.

INFORMATION PROCESSING LEARNING THEORY

Information processing learning theory (IPLT) has ample research support from educational and memory research but also from neuroscientists who study brain functioning and the effects of brain damage. IPLT has strong explanatory power and predicts many learning principles. Due to its solid and extensive empirical support from different lines of research, IPLT is one of the best and most accepted theories of learning.

IPLT describes human learning in terms of functional information *storage types* (i.e., types of memories) and basic *processes* that transform information and control the mental flow of information among the types of memories. At its most general level, IPLT describes human learning via two processes: *encoding* of information as knowledge in the brain and *retrieval* of that knowledge to support behavior and thinking.

Sensed information is processed (i.e., transformed) into stored mental representations (knowledge) that guide current and future behavior. IPLT provides details about how encoding and retrieval work in terms of specific subprocesses and storage functions.

Early memory models, such as the modal memory model of Atkinson and Shiffrin (1968), identified three types of functional memory storage with distinct characteristics: sensory store, short-term memory (STM), and long-term memory (LTM). Various *control processes* act on information in these storage structures to determine what and how information is encoded as knowledge and retrieved to guide behavior.

MEMORY STORE TYPES

Research has indicated four *types of memory storage* that differ functionally in how much information each can store and how long information is retained. Intermediate memory can be added to the three types of the modal memory model. Characteristics of the memory types explain several learning principles.

Sensory Store

The *sensory store* holds representations sensed by our five senses (we have sensory stores for each sense). Sensory memory can store large amounts of information (e.g., our entire visual field) for very short times.

Information represented in the sensory store is the source of potential representations in short-term memory. The operation of sensory memory is quite automatic and fast and, if working properly, has few principles of concern to instructors.

Short-Term and Working Memory

Short-term memory (STM) holds information from our sensory store that we consciously think about. The capacity of STM is very low—only a few units of information. Information also fades from STM after a few seconds. When information is consciously processed in STM, researchers refer to "working memory" (WM).

Examples of conscious processing include mental math or mentally repeating a phone number. Our *working memory capacity* (WMC) is very small. When we are thinking hard about something (or the mental task is more difficult), we are able to store only a few items of information. This limited capacity makes paper and pencil very useful for processing more information.

The characteristics of WM result in several learning principles. For example, WM is used in solving math problems in our heads. WM retrieves knowledge from LTM about math operations we learned previously and also holds newly sensed information such as the actual numbers involved in a specific problem. WM is then used to apply the operations to the specific numbers to find an answer. The process and the numbers must be stored in WM.

Because WM processing requires effort, people generally avoid using WM until they cannot solve a problem by simple recall or effortless intuition (i.e., unconscious automatic processing). The amount of effort required to do a conscious mental task is also called *cognitive load* by some researchers.

A major task of instructors is to convince students to do effortful processing to encode information in LTM (i.e., to learn). Processing information longer, repeatedly, or in specific ways makes encoding in LTM more likely. If the cognitive load of the learning task is low, people learn more quickly and easily. Intentional effortful processing is important for formal learning, and therefore characteristics of WM are often the focus of learning and instructional theory.

Different WM is associated with each of our different senses. WM for visual information is different than WM for auditory information. These memories are independent, so using one does not affect the other. Processing information in multiple types of WM at the same time decreases cognitive load, resulting in a principle about the increased instructional effectiveness of presenting both visual and auditory information.

Intermediate-Term Memory

Some evidence from neuroscience and psychology supports an intermediate-term memory (ITM) that stores information for longer periods than STM and is involved in formation of LTM. ITM holds information longer than STM, but the information can be forgotten, unlike information in LTM. ITM is missing from many models of memory, including standard IPLT models.

Educational evidence for ITM derives from the observation that students score better on assessments of learning if assessed shortly compared to longer delays before assessment. Evidence from neuroscience comes from study of the memory performance of animals with damaged brain areas associated with the encoding in LTM. Such animals display learning for short periods only.

LTM storage is thought to occur over time via a consolidation process that moves information from a more volatile and effortful ITM to a more permanent LTM. How the consolidation process occurs and what parts of the brain are involved is a matter of active research, though it has been suggested that sleep is involved. Too little is known about the consolidation process to serve as a basis for instructional principles beyond the recommendation that instructors allow sufficient time for consolidation and that practice of recall and use over longer time periods likely supports learning.

Long-Term Memory

LTM stores huge amounts of information for very long periods, which can be retrieved to guide behavior and support processing in working memory. What we call knowledge is information represented in LTM. Getting specific knowledge (specified as learning outcomes or standards) into LTM is therefore the primary goal of formal education. Researchers have categorized such knowledge into types.

TYPES OF KNOWLEDGE IN LTM

Scientists have identified two general types of stored long-term memories: declarative and nondeclarative. *Declarative memories* (also called explicit memories) can be intentionally recalled and often involve symbolic representation like language. A subtype of declarative memory is *semantic memory*—memory of concepts and ideas that can be summarized as "knowing that," for example, knowing that George Washington is the name of the first president of the United States. Semantic memories are, of course, very important for achieving educational goals.

Humans also store nondeclarative memories (*implicit knowledge*) that we cannot verbalize, including procedures and skills like how to

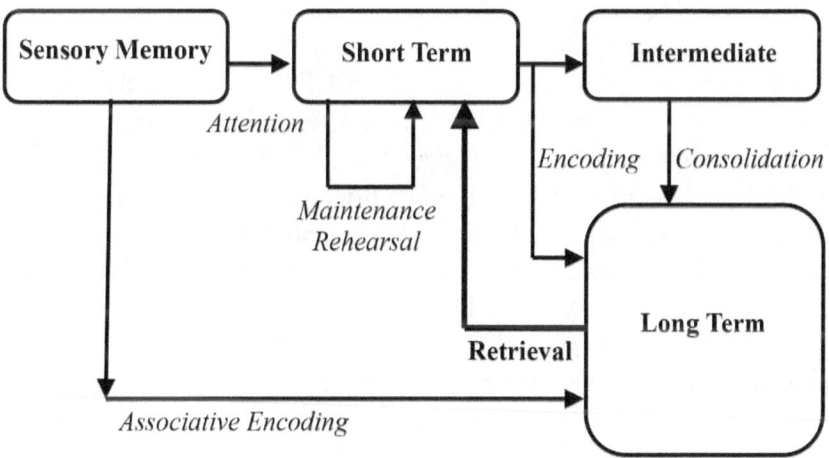

Figure 4.1. Information Processing Model of Memories and Control Processes

ride a bike or tie a shoelace. *Procedural memories* are nondeclarative memories about "knowing how" (but not explaining how—that is declarative). Using (i.e., retrieving) nondeclarative memories tends to be effortless and automatic and does not involve language or symbols.

Learning procedures may initially require much effort and attention (and reference to semantic knowledge), but eventually procedures become *automatized* with practice. For example, driving a car or tying a shoelace at first requires much conscious effort and reference to semantic information about how to do each task. After several repetitions, the task is automatized. Such automatized procedures require little conscious effort to use.

SEMANTIC NETWORKS

Semantic knowledge is a major goal of formal education. Target semantic knowledge is expressed as learning outcomes, for example, in state learning standards. The processing of semantic information is generally effortful and conscious, involving processing by working memory.

Semantic memories are associated with (i.e., linked to) other related representations, forming a network of linked representations that establish meaning. For example, the concept bird is associated with the word "bird," with sounds birds make, with flight, and with feathers, which establish the meaning of the concept. Such associations are established at the time of learning based on information in the learning environment and a learner's prior knowledge.

The associational network structure of LTM is an essential characteristic of human knowledge that affects how students learn, including the importance of prior knowledge. The linked representations that establish meaning result in important principles for both encoding of new information and retrieval of knowledge. Students tend to store new knowledge by incorporating it into an existing network of associations (called schema by some researchers).

Meaning is very important in understanding how humans learn. Humans tend to recall the gist or meaning of information rather than a detailed copy of sensed information (i.e., rote knowledge). Learners tend to better store and retrieve meaningful information because such information is linked to other information that promotes encoding and retrieval. Humans can more easily recall information that they link to their existing knowledge.

When students recall specific knowledge, they retrieve other information associated with the knowledge. When a student recalls the concept of a bird, she also accesses other associated information. Such information is "activated" or retrieved into working memory.

The facts, concepts, and principles found in typical target learning outcomes are semantic knowledge. The performance of a procedure, however, is nondeclarative memory. An effective model of instruction seeks principles that relate types of instructional methods to learning these types of memories/outcomes. For example, a primary learning principle is that newly sensed information that fits into existing knowledge is easier to learn than information that requires changes to current knowledge or creation of an entirely new schema.

The associational nature of semantic knowledge in LTM makes changing concepts much more difficult that learning new concepts. The web of associations resists change even if new information contradicts existing knowledge. If new information results in a change, the old associations work overtime to restore the changed knowledge back into its old form. This gradual spontaneous restoration of prior knowledge makes conceptual change very difficult to achieve by instruction.

HIGHER-ORDER KNOWLEDGE

Higher-order knowledge refers to learning outcomes such as reasoning, critical thinking, and novel problem solving. Higher-order outcomes are represented by the discover/generate use level of learning taxonomy presented in chapter 1. Such skills and abilities involve conceptual and procedural knowledge, but they also involve cognitive control features and processes such as retrieval speed and working memory capacity. Such features and processes, not being knowledge, are very difficult (or impossible) to improve by instruction.

Teaching relevant knowledge such as concepts, principles, and procedures that are necessary for reasoning, critical thinking, and problem solving does support higher-order learning. Instruction, however, does not ensure general improvement in cognitive abilities. Practice of higher-order tasks likely will improve a students' use of their cognitive processing potential (in a specific context). However, because instruction is likely not effective in changing mental processes and abilities, it is difficult to link specific instructional strategies to improved higher-order processing.

COGNITIVE PROCESSES

In addition to types of memories, IPLT describes processes that transform mental representations of information for long-term storage and retrieval. Cognitive control processes underlie individual student differences in learning speed and reasoning. These processes explain many learning principles, such as the difficulty students having in learning large amounts of new information.

Whether instruction can affect cognitive control processes is controversial. In general, evidence indicates that instruction does not affect such processes. This lack of evidence should be considered before paying for mental exercises that are touted as improving cognitive performance.

The overarching cognitive processes are the encoding of sensed information and the retrieval of knowledge to guide actions and thinking. These general processes comprise several subprocesses identified by IPLT.

Encoding

Encoding is the process of adding or changing representations in LTM—transforming sensed information into knowledge. Encoding need not be conscious (e.g., implicit memories, incidental learning, and conditioning) and therefore need not involve working memory. Learning of interest for education, however, often does involve conscious processing. So the focus for most instruction is the processing of semantic information in working memory.

Consolidation

Memory researchers describe a *consolidation* process in which some newly learned knowledge becomes fixed in LTM over time. Once knowledge is consolidated, it can be directly used from LTM without the conscious effort involved in using working memory to retrieve and process the information. Using such automatized knowledge is less effortful and conscious. For example, people do not have to think about their route home from work. Unfortunately, this consolidation process, which is key to very long-term storage and easy use of knowledge, is currently not well understood, so few principles can be stated for this process.

Retrieval

Retrieval is the process of recalling knowledge from LTM to working memory for processing resulting in behavior and thinking. Retrieval of semantic knowledge involves generative and constructive processes. Retrieved memories are constructed, or made up, rather than just recalled.

An important point for instruction is that retrieval of knowledge itself can alter knowledge and thus result in learning. Repetition of retrieval of specific information makes that information easier to retrieve. Moreover, retrieval can result in reorganization of knowledge, including new associations. This process is the basis of learning by externalization.

Attention

Because not all sensed information is stored in STM, some process must filter information from the sensory store to STM. That process is *attention*, which can be controlled voluntarily or directed by sensory events such as loud noises. As we can consciously process only the information that gets into working memory, only information that students attend to can be the basis of learning typical educational goals. Attention is therefore a critical process affecting school learning. The associated learning principle is that increased attention results in better learning.

Students are not conscious of all information to which they are attending. Research indicates that learners learn many things they are unaware of (cannot say they sensed or learned), which is *incidental learning* as opposed to *intentional learning*. So, while attention improves learning, awareness of what is learned is not required. The way information is processed affects learning more than the reason such processing occurred. This means that, for example, whether students attend to information matters more than students' goal in processing the information.

What variables affect conscious attention? Some sensory information is inherently more attention grabbing than other information. People pay attention to some types of information, such as morbid, sexual, or life-threatening content. Information that contradicts or challenges existing knowledge also has the potential of gaining attention, at least initially. Other information may be of more or less interest based on students' age, developmental level, or culture. Individual students will display greater attention to information that is meaningful to them (i.e., for which they already have schema).

Attention affects retrieval by determining which sensory cues are consciously processed. So attention also plays a role in knowledge retrieval in addition to encoding.

Rehearsal Processes

Other control processes affect representations in working memory. *Maintenance rehearsal* is mentally repeating information to keep it in STM. Maintenance rehearsal control processes are thought to affect whether STM representations are encoded in LTM and so are important for learning. For example, mentally repeating a historical fact in WM increases the likelihood that the fact will be encoded.

Elaborative rehearsal is a merging in WM of newly sensed information with prior knowledge. Effectively, learners generate (i.e., make up) new knowledge that incorporates the new information with what they already know. The newly elaborated knowledge can be easily added to an existing schema, and it is therefore the basis of learning. Elaborative rehearsal is why prior knowledge is so important for learning. New information can be learned rote via maintenance rehearsal, but elaboration based on what the learner already knows is the basis for most learning of semantic information.

Executive Functions

Executive functions are associated with planning, problem solving, logic, inhibiting automatic responses, and goal-directed behavior. These functions generally involve intentional and conscious processing of information in working memory. Neuroscientists have noticed these functions are reduced in patients with damage to frontal lobes of the brain, a brain region that integrates information from various parts of the brain and also regulates and controls other brain functions.

From an information-processing perspective, executive functions are control processes that direct and coordinate mental processing to achieve goals, including solving problems. Such executive processes are therefore associated with higher-order learning outcomes.

LEVELS OF PROCESSING

Craik and Lockhart (1972) proposed a *levels-of-processing principle* that links how information is mentally processed to how well it is learned. When learners are told to do different tasks with the information, some tasks result in better recall of the information. For example, in memorizing a list of words, some learners are told to count the number of the letter "e" in each word; others are told to think of a synonym. Those thinking of a synonym are able to recall more words when tested.

Instructors, therefore, should favor some types of processing. Tasks that require more processing, especially processing related to meaning, result in better learning. The better performance with semantic tasks underscores the importance of meaning and prior knowledge for learning.

However, the *transfer appropriate processing principle* states that better learning occurs when the encoding process better matches the process guiding retrieval. In other words, students better retrieve knowledge via a process that is similar to the process used to learn the knowledge.

For example, Morris and colleagues (1977) found that learners that attended to rhyming features of words did better than learners attending to word meaning when asked to identify words that rhymed with previous words. A similar *encoding specificity principle* of Tulving and Thompson (1973) states that a learner's ability to recall information depends on the similarity of the encoding and retrieval processing.

INTERNALIZATION AND EXTERNALIZATION OF INFORMATION

The primary processes of memory encoding and retrieval relate to the two key processes of formal learning involved with achievement of typical learning outcomes: *internalization* of information as knowledge and *externalization* of knowledge as information. Internalization involves transformation of sensed information into stored knowledge typical for educational goals. Externalization involves the transformation of knowledge into external (often symbolic) information. Different cognitive control processes are associated with each process making them different in terms of ideal instructional support.

Traditional IPLT focuses primarily on internalization. Learning researchers have focused on how humans and other animals process new information into knowledge. The control processes of IPLT are specified from the perspective of what promotes internalization (i.e., encoding). Educators also sometimes treat internalization as the only learning process, as, for example, when educators see lecturing alone as an instructional method.

The externalization process also results in learning. The process of retrieving knowledge, organizing it as externalized information, and translating the knowledge into an external representation can result in knowledge reorganization and creation.

Traditional instructional practice has long recognized the importance of externalization for learning. Quizzes and homework assignments that require students to externalize their knowledge are common

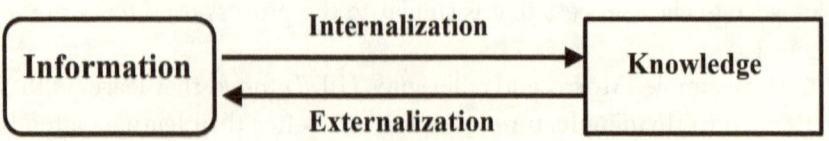

Figure 4.2. Key Learning Processes

components of instruction. Unfortunately, few learning theories or research studies have identified the basic cognitive processes involved with learning by externalization.

Viewing instruction from the perspective of supporting internalization and externalization can improve instructional planning and effectiveness. Some internalization of new information is always involved in instruction, but supporting externalization is also required, no matter how well the information is presented. Instructional methods should specify support for both processes. What instructors can do to promote both internalization and externalization is a major focus of subsequent chapters.

THIS CHAPTER IN A NUTSHELL

A valid (i.e., evidence-based) learning theory provides the basis for improving instruction because it explains how students learn. This chapter presents the IPLT that explains and predicts multiple important learning principles and is supported by basic research about how our cognitive system works (see table 4.1). Different types of memory are described along with various cognitive processes that transform mental representations of information. Two general learning processes: internalization and externalization provide the basis for a useful instructional model described in the next chapter.

Many learning principles can be derived from IP theory that can serve as a basis for instruction, including:

Table 4.1. Important Learning Principles

Prior Knowledge	New semantic information that aligns with a learner's prior knowledge is more readily learned.
Small Amounts of Information	Allowing learners time to process small amounts of information more frequently promotes learning compared to presenting large amounts of information before allowing time to process.
Multiple Senses	Information from multiple senses is more readily processed and learned.
Attention	Students who devote more attention to information learn it faster.
Meaningful Information	Processing for meaning during encoding results in better semantic learning.
Retrieval Practice	Retrieval practice improves recall performance.

Retrieval Learning	Retrieval of knowledge can result in new knowledge. Generation of information during recall results in better learning than attending to new information.
Conceptual Change	Changing prior knowledge is much more difficult than adding new knowledge.
Intention to Learn	People learn many things they do not intend to learn. Intention to learn does not by itself improve learning.

QUESTIONS

1. Connect one of the principles in table 4.1 to your own instruction by explaining how the principle guides your instructional actions.
2. Do all students mainly learn the same way or all learn differently? List the ways they are alike and/or different in how they learn.
3. How do you think the limitations of short-term/working memory affect learning? What do the limitations suggest instructors should do in presenting information for internalization?
4. What is the source of most information people encounter? Into what categories can these sources be classified? Are some categories more important than others?
5. How important for formal education is procedural knowledge compared to declarative knowledge? Do most state standards address processes or declarative knowledge? Keep in mind that learning processes often do not involve knowing a list of process steps—consider learning to tie a shoelace.
6. What is the source of most of students' semantic knowledge: experience, visual images from media such as video, or symbolic information such as text?

REFERENCES

Atkinson, R. C., and R. M. Shiffrin. "Human Memory: A Proposed System and Its Control Processes." In *The Psychology of Learning and Motivation: Advances in Research and Theory Vol. 2*, edited by K. W. Spence and J. T. Spence, 89–195. New York: Academic Press, 1968.

Craik, Fergus I. M., and Robert S. Lockhart. "Levels of Processing: A Framework for Memory Research." *Journal of Verbal Learning and Verbal Behavior* 11.6 (1972) 671–84.

Morris, C. D., J. D Bransford, and J. J. Franks. "Levels of Processing versus Transfer-Appropriate Processing." *Journal of Verbal Learning and Verbal Behavior* 16 (1977): 519–33.

Pinker, Steven. *How the Mind Works*. New York: Norton, 1997.
Squire, Larry R. "Memory Systems of the Brain: A Brief History and Current Perspective." *Neurobiology of Learning and Memory* 82, no. 3 (2004): 171–77.
Tulving, Endel, and Donald M. Thomson. "Encoding Specificity and Retrieval Processes in Episodic Memory." *Psychological Review* 80, no. 5 (1973): 352–73.

5

AN INFORMATION PROCESSING INSTRUCTIONAL MODEL

What this chapter is about: Presents a new model of instruction that indicates what matters for increased instructional effectiveness.
Why this matters: A model of instruction indicates what is important for improving instructional quality in all instructional situations.

Some confusion exists among both educators and researchers about the difference between learning theory and instructional theory. The popular tendency to label instruction as learning (e.g., cooperative learning, project-based learning, etc.) contributes to the confusion. Learning theories concern how people learn. Instructional theories (or models) indicate what instructors should do to promote targeted learning.

The relationship of a learning theory to an instructional model is similar to the relationship between a physical theory and engineering tasks. For example, physical theory involving forces and material strength is the basis for a model that guides engineers in building bridges. Likewise, an instructional model relies on learning theory to guide instructional actions. The analogy is apt because instructors are very much like engineers of learning.

Comprehensive instructional models prescribe or recommend how to promote targeted learning for specific students in specific contexts. An instructional model should include qualifiers about aspects of specific instructional situations that indicate conditions under which principles are valid. *Universal* instructional principles work for all outcomes and all students in all instructional environments, but other principles should specify for what learning outcomes, and for which students, the principle applies.

Instructional recommendations must be practical. Instructional models are intended for instructor use and therefore should be oriented to typical instructor knowledge and terminology. Principles of the model should use concepts and terminology familiar to instructors rather than terminology familiar to learning researchers.

An instructional model guides the creation of an instructional design—a plan specifying instructional strategies and methods to help students learn target outcomes. Instructional strategies are general features of instruction thought to promote learning based on learning principles. For example, a curriculum designer might employ a strategy of high-learner control throughout a curriculum. Instructional methods are specific procedures that employ strategies. An instructional designer might choose to use a reciprocal teaching method at a specific point within a course.

Previously proposed instructional models include Robert Gagne's Conditions of Learning or Charles Reigeluth's Elaboration Theory. These models tend to focus on the organization of instructional events, particularly the sequence of information presentation. Other proposed models (e.g., discovery learning, project-based learning) tend to focus on achieving a specific type of learning goal (in these examples, the skill of self-directed learning) and downplay other types of learning.

Both models model include a learning taxonomy, but Gagne's model also includes the idea of a *learning hierarchy*. High-level learning outcomes, such as ones found in state standards, are further specified in terms of component outcomes that are smaller learning tasks required for the higher outcome. Such a hierarchy indicates what must be learned prerequisite to achieving a targeted learning outcome and suggests a sequence of simpler component learning tasks.

An instructional model gets much of its empirical validity from the learning theory on which it is based. The learning theory foundation of these instructional models is not explicitly identified, raising questions about the empirical soundness of the models. These models are helpful, but instructors need a comprehensive and flexible model of instruction based on empirically sound learning theory.

AN I-E INSTRUCTIONAL MODEL

A model of instruction based on information processing learning theory (IPLT) focuses on strategies and methods that support the information internalization and externalization processes. Principles of the *I-E instructional model* specify how to optimize information selection and presentation to support internalization and also how to support externalization with learning activities.

Instructional designers and instructors designate information for students via sources such as textbooks and video clips. Instructors provide access to resources via different media but also present information themselves by, for example, lecturing or conducting discussions.

Instructors also support externalization by assigning learning activities. Doing learning activities is not about having students listen to, read, or observe information, though students may need to do so in doing the activity. Learning activities require students to use or apply their knowledge. Requiring a student to answer questions is a simple externalization task, so is having students do lengthy, complex, or "authentic" projects. Learning activities focus on student expression of their knowledge as information so others can interpret the information.

A complete instructional method should support both learning processes by specifying which and how information will be presented and also what learning activities students are expected to do. By this definition, simply presenting information without externalization is not a complete instructional method. Merely lecturing students, assigning readings, or viewing a video is not a valid instructional method. Assigning learning activities without providing supporting information is also not a complete instructional method.

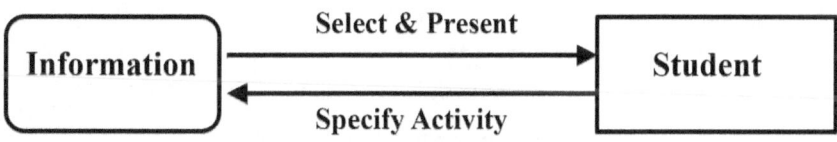

Figure 5.1.   Instructional Model

LEARNING VARIABLES

The starting point for instructional prescription is identification of learning variables—characteristics of instructional goals, environments, or students that have evidence of affecting learning. Principles of IPLT indicate learning variables and suggest how the variables should be set to promote and improve learning and better achieve instructional goals.

According to the Carroll Model of School Learning (Carroll 1989), the key variable of learning is *time to learn* (TTL, see figure 5.2). Students vary in how long it takes them to learn specific outcomes. Carroll suggested major learning variables that affect students' TTL including: aptitude, ability to understand, and perseverance—all variables of students. Carroll also identified a fourth variable affecting TTL: instructional quality.

Carroll's model indicates that instruction can be optimized for all students by simply giving each student all the time they need to learn target outcomes. In other words, optimal instruction should be individualized based on time needed to learn.

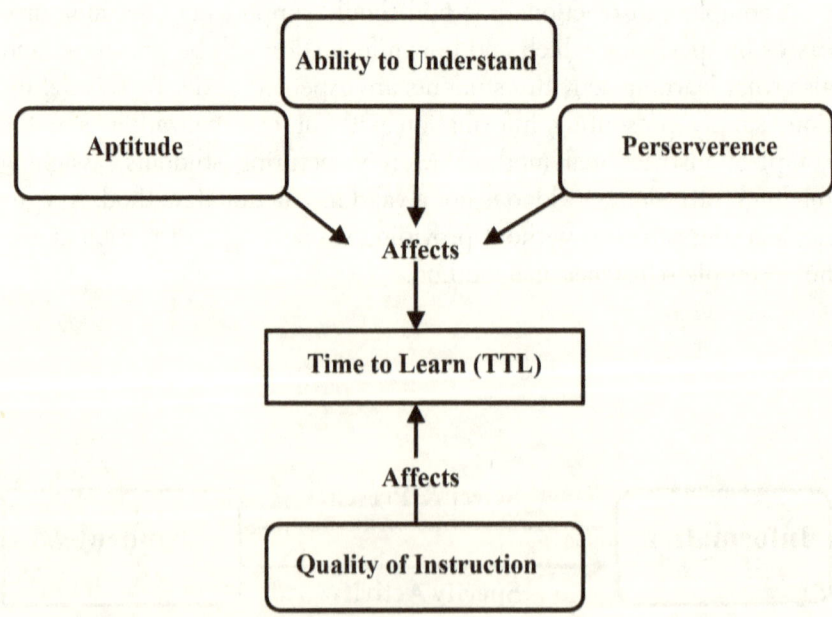

Figure 5.2. Carroll Model of School Learning

Unfortunately, for practical reasons, our historical educational model is based on group instruction (i.e., classes) over fixed time intervals (semesters, units, etc.). This model does not support individualized instruction based on TTL. The task of instruction in typical schools is to get the maximum number of students to achieve targeted learning objectives within an allotted time period. Instructors therefore seek to set learning variables to achieve that goal.

From Carroll's perspective, some students are not being given an *opportunity to learn* because they are not given sufficient time to learn. Instructors attempt to provide sufficient opportunity to learn by giving some students additional learning time, but the amount of time available for remedial instruction is very limited. Instructional programs such as the multi-tiered system of supports (MTSS) provide additional instructional time and methods for students who do not achieve targeted learning within the time allotted in the typical classroom.

> **INDIVIDUALIZATION PRINCIPLE—RELEVANCE**
> Providing sufficient time to learning maximizes learning for each student.

STUDENT LEARNING VARIABLES: ABILITY, PRIOR KNOWLEDGE, AND PERSEVERANCE

Students vary greatly in their learning ability, meaning they vary in the time needed to learn, even if other learning variables are equal (i.e., the students have equal knowledge, perseverance, and quality of instruction). Learning ability has various labels including aptitude, cognitive ability, general intelligence, or fluid intelligence. A popular buzz phrase is that "all students can learn." In fact, all animals can learn, but this phrase ignores the fact that students learn at very different rates.

IPLT explains differences in learner ability through differences in cognitive functioning. For example, learners vary in the number of items they can store in short-term memory (their memory span) and working memory capacity. Learning ability greatly affects TTL, but instructors can do little about student learning aptitude. The question of interest to instructors is whether students with different learning ability respond differently to different instructional methods.

What Carroll calls "ability to understand" is about what students already know—their prior knowledge. Students with fewer schema related to the instructional content cannot learn that content as quickly as those with more prior knowledge. Practically, students who have less knowledge of a topic need more time to learn. The existing schemata of students greatly affect their TTL. Instructors can do nothing about students lacking prior knowledge other than take time to teach it, which increases time to learn the target outcomes.

Carroll's perseverance variable is similar to student motivation. Carroll more precisely defines this variable as the amount of time a student attends to instruction. Such attention is often seen as dependent on the amount of effort a student is willing to devote to learning an outcome. Such effort is attributed to student interest in the topic or their industry in the face of disinterest or difficulty ("grit" is the current buzzword). A student whose attention wanders or who "gives up" more easily needs more time to learn. What an instructor can do to increase student perseverance is an open question for instructional theory.

Instructors have little or no control of student variables. Instructors do, however, control the values of many environmental learning variables. Therefore, setting environmental variables to lessen TTL is the primary means of improving instructional quality.

ENVIRONMENTAL LEARNING VARIABLES

Environmental learning variables are aspects of the instructional environment that affect TTL. Such variables are potential differences of the learning situation experienced by students, not differences in students themselves. For example, instructors control what information is presented to students, how it is presented, what students are expected to do with the information, and what type of feedback is given to students. How instructors set the values of such variables determines the instructional methods students experience and therefore determines instructional quality.

Some environmental learning variables improve TTL for all students. Other such variables have different effects based on student differences. For example, different instructional methods may affect TTL differently for students of different ability. The task of instructors is to optimally set environmental learning variables and also adjust such variables based on student learning variables.

The magnitude of improved learning (i.e., reduced TTL) we can expect from improved instructional quality is small compared to the effect that student variables have on TTL (see chapter 1). Improved instruction, therefore, *cannot completely compensate for differences in students*. Beware of claims that any instructional technique, method, or environment can level the playing field for all students.

OTHER IP-BASED INSTRUCTIONAL MODELS

Principles of IPLT that indicate which environmental learning variables promote learning are discussed in succeeding chapters. Some instructional models other than the I-E model are based on IPLT and provide useful learning principles.

The cognitive load theory of John Sweller (1988) focuses on a *cognitive load* construct as a means for guiding instruction. Cognitive load is the mental effort required to process information for internalization. From this perspective, instructors seek to minimize cognitive load in order to reduce time to learn.

Cognitive load theory references the limitations of short-term and working memory as the basis of the mental effort required to internalize information. *Intrinsic cognitive load* is due to the inherent difficulty of presented information (calculus requires more effort than addition). *Extraneous cognitive load* is due to how information is presented, so it is the type of cognitive load that higher-quality instruction can reduce. Efforts to improve instruction therefore focus on setting variables of information presentation to reduce extraneous cognitive load. Cognitive load theory is focused on internalization and does not provide much guidance for supporting externalization.

Multimedia learning theory (MMLT) is an instructional model (despite the name) developed by Richard E. Mayer and Roxana Moreno (1998). MMLT identifies principles of how to present information via multiple media to enhance internalization. MMLT theory includes a list of evidence-based principles that promote internalization and lessen time to learn.

For example, an MMLT principle states that presentation of information via multiple sensory modes better promotes learning than using a single sensory mode. This principle results from the independence of the types of working memory for different sensory modes. Like cognitive load theory, MMLT is focused on internalization rather than the externalization process.

SUMMARY OF INSTRUCTIONAL MODELS

Improved instruction can lessen the time needed for students to learn (in other words, improve learning). To improve instruction, instructors must set the values of environmental learning variables to better promote learning. While some previous instructional models contain principles for improved information presentation based on IPLT, the I-E instructional model specifies more principles (and therefore variables) for promoting internalization and externalization.

QUESTIONS

1. Explain the difference between a learning theory and an instructional theory to a colleague.
2. Write down some of the instructional methods you use in your instruction. Identify how the methods set variables that support internalization and externalization.
3. How do you deal with students who do not learn targeted outcomes within the allotted time of your instruction? What are some alternatives?
4. What concepts or procedures do your administrators or colleagues promote for improving instruction? What (and how much) evidence supports these concepts? What learning theory supports these concepts?
5. Does your organization promote concepts or methods intended to compensate for student differences? Discuss with another in-

structor whether ability grouping compensates for student differences.
6. What do you think instructors can do to gain the attention of more than twenty students with different knowledge, interests, and dispositions?

REFERENCES

Carroll, John B. "The Carroll Model: A 25-Year Retrospective and Prospective View." *Educational Researcher* 18, no. 1 (1989): 26.

Mayer, R. E., and R. Moreno. "A Cognitive Theory of Multimedia Learning: Implications for Design Principles" (1998). http://www.unm.edu/~moreno/PDFS/chi.pdf.

Mayer, Richard E. *Multimedia Learning*. Cambridge: Cambridge University Press, 2001.

Sweller, John. "Cognitive Load during Problem Solving: Effects on Learning." *Cognitive Science* 12, no. 2 (1988): 257–85.

6

INSTRUCTIONAL SUPPORT FOR INTERNALIZATION

What this chapter is about: This chapter identifies variables controlled by instructors that can affect students' time to internalize information.
Why that matters: Internalization is the primary learning process. Students must internalize information to meet most learning goals and also as a precursor to externalization.

Internalization of sensed information into knowledge has long been recognized as the primary learning process. It is the only process of nonhuman animal learning. Internalization is synonymous with learning in many learning theories, including the information processing learning theory (IPLT). Learning theories tend to treat internalization as the only learning process that need be explained.

During internalization, the learner is passive in the sense that he or she does not interact with the source of the information beyond perceiving and mentally processing the information. Information flow is one-way from the information source to the learner. Students are quite capable of learning via internalization only as demonstrated by learning from books and online video clips or simply observing instructors.

Limitation in the amount of information that can be processed in working memory is a major factor influencing internalization. IPLT also indicates that internalization is supported by maintenance rehearsal (i.e., repeated mental practice) or elaborative rehearsal in which new information is associated with prior knowledge. Evidence indicates that meaningful information (i.e., that which can be linked to prior knowledge) is better internalized.

Instructors support internalization in two ways: by selecting *what* information is presented and by determining *how* that information is presented to students. Instructors determine the content of the information presented and also how that information is made available to students. The way to improved instruction for internalization is to select information and sources based on principles that link learning variables to better internalization. Such principles are suggested by IPLT and expressed in the I-E instructional model.

Instructors must analyze their instructional needs and carefully consider alternatives to lessen time to internalize. Defaulting to lectures and textbook readings because they are convenient or traditional ways to present information is unlikely to result in optimal instruction. Presentation methods should be used judiciously, selected based on their learning variable characteristics rather than because of tradition or ease of implementation. An instructor must consider the functioning and limitations of the human cognitive system, as stated in IPLT, to determine how to set learning variables to optimize internalization.

LEARNING VARIABLES OF INFORMATION SELECTION

While people other than instructors typically determine target learning outcomes, selection of information presented in support of those outcomes is often the responsibility of the instructor. Letting textbook

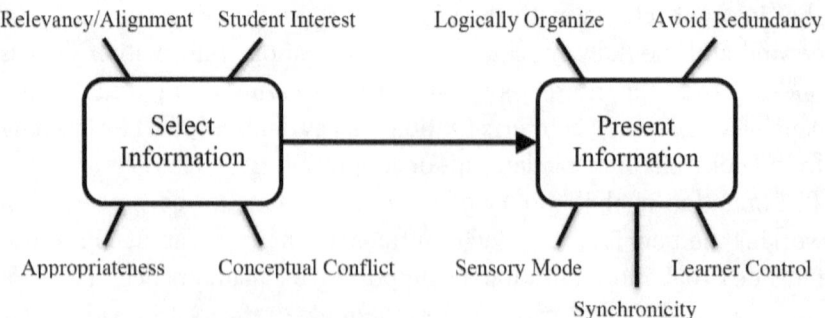

Figure 6.1. Supporting Internalization

writers or other product creators determine what information is presented to students is not ideal as such authors are often unaware of what learning outcomes are expected. Letting students select information themselves is very risky because students are often unable to identify relevant or appropriate information.

Instructors should consider key environmental learning variables to improve internalization. Such variables include the relevance, appropriateness, learner interest, and the amount of conceptual conflict present in information.

Relevance

Instructional designers obviously should select information relevant for promoting targeted learning outcomes. Instructors judge whether information is relevant by assessing how well information aligns with targeted learning outcomes. Irrelevant or off-the-point information has been shown to make internalization more difficult because irrelevant information can draw student attention away from relevant information.

> **SELECTION PRINCIPLE—RELEVANCE**
> Presenting only information relevant to the targeted learning outcomes decreases time to internalize. Information that is unrelated to the outcome but thought to increase motivation or attention is often detrimental to learning.

Student Interest

Instructors should select relevant information thought to better hold the attention of targeted students. Information that gains and holds attention can affect student perseverance. Specific examples and contexts of information may be interesting to students at a specific developmental level or from a specific cultural background.

This variable is sometimes oversold, at it is often difficult to find information that is interesting to all students in a class. Students vary in what they are interested in. What interests some may not have high interest for others. Selecting interesting information for a group of students is a hit-or-miss proposition for the individual students. "Making" information interesting is easier said than done.

Including information that is interesting to students but unrelated to the learning outcome, in an effort to increase attention, is generally counterproductive because students attend to that information at the expense of the relevant information. Instructors should avoid seductive details that are very interesting to most students but do not promote internalization of targeted outcomes.

> **SELECTION PRINCIPLE—STUDENT INTEREST**
> Presenting information that is of higher interest to students results in greater attention and less time to internalize.

Appropriateness (Suitability to Students)

Selected information should also be chosen based on whether the information is appropriate for the development level and background of the student audience, in other words, whether the information matches the characteristics of targeted students. For example, the reading level of text information should match the grade level of students. Selected information should also match the prior knowledge of students, including their cultural knowledge. Information that uses culturally familiar examples, for example, can reduce time to internalize.

> **SELECTION PRINCIPLE—APPROPRIATENESS**
> Presenting information appropriate for the demographics of target students decreases time to internalize.

Conceptual Conflict

Presenting information that challenges students' existing knowledge and beliefs causes *conceptual conflict* that is useful for achieving many learning outcomes. The cognitive discomfort that such information arouses in students can stimulate their cognitive processing to resolve the conflict, increasing the likelihood of internalization. Establishing if or what students already believe, and how that is different from targeted outcomes, enables instructors to select information likely to cause conceptual conflict.

Students sometimes respond to information that conflicts with their beliefs by simply dismissing and ignoring such information. This response obviously does not promote increased processing, so merely providing conflicting information is insufficient for improving instruction. Changing beliefs involves conceptual change, which is difficult to accomplish.

> **SELECTION PRINCIPLE—CONCEPTUAL CONFLICT**
> Presenting information that challenges or contradicts a students' prior knowledge, naive beliefs, and expectations can stimulate attention and processing for internalization and conceptual change.

INFORMATION SELECTION FOR CONCEPTUAL CHANGE

Internalization is the creation of a new schema or the extension of an existing schema to include new associations based on new information. Conceptual change is another type of internalization that changes the associations of an existing schema.

Causing conceptual change is much more difficult than establishing new knowledge that does not contradict a student's existing beliefs. The best current prescription for conceptual change is for instructors to assess students' current beliefs regarding targeted outcomes, to adapt the presentation to include and challenge those beliefs, and to allow more instructional time and effort if targeted outcomes involve conceptual change.

Presenting information that causes conceptual conflict can support conceptual change. But how such information is presented can affect how well students respond to the conflict. Likely, increased guidance involving scripted externalization can help. Revisiting concepts taught previously maximizes the chance that existing beliefs will change, suggesting that curricula that regularly review previous instruction are better for inducing conceptual change.

LEARNING VARIABLES OF INFORMATION PRESENTATION

Several evidence-based principles indicate how information presentation can be optimized to support internalization. From the perspective of cognitive load theory, for example, specific ways of presenting information can lessen the *extraneous cognitive load*. Researchers have also studied how to improve presentation of visual information (e.g., techniques recommended by Edward Tufte) and text (e.g., *information mapping*) to improve speed of internalization.

Digital technology has made the presentation of information via multiple and dynamic media more efficient and available. Multimedia learning theory (MMLT) prescribes principles for arranging information on video screens to improve internalization. Digital documents can also include the use of *hypertext* (linked information), which offers new methods to present information in adaptable ways that are under student control.

Specific guidance of how instructors should arrange information in creating slide presentations, tutorials, and supportive text documents can be found from sources mentioned above. The variables listed below result from more general presentation principles derived from IPLT that provide a broad basis for improving internalization.

Amount and Organization of Presented Information

Despite the increasing amount and diversity of information included in textbooks and the pressure on instructors for topic "coverage," a key presentation principle is that presenting less information and allowing sufficient time for processing results in quicker internalization. Due to limitations in working memory capacity, humans can process only small amounts of information within a time period typical of instruction. Too much information will overload the working memory of students, so in general, less information is better.

The structure or organization of presented information is a variable that previous instruction models (e.g., Gagne's Conditions of Learning) have stressed. Most models agree that initially presenting the goals of the presentation (i.e., the learning objectives) is beneficial. Theorists also suggest that a logical sequence of information from simple and stand-alone subtopics to more complex and dependent ones aids learning. A review or summary at the end of the presentation also helps students retain the information. The work of Rosenshine and Stevens (1986) is a resource suggesting details of information presentation structure, as is the elaboration theory of Charles Reigeluth.

For example, presentation arranged in a hierarchy of more general concepts with subordinate specific topics promotes understanding. Presentation sequences of first general and foundational information and later more elaborated information tend to promote internalization.

> **PRESENTATION PRINCIPLE—AMOUNT AND ORGANIZATION**
> Time to internalize decreases when presented information is logically organized into small chunks.

Redundancy

Repeating information during presentation is generally not helpful as it increases cognitive load. Instead, repeating key information at later times helps consolidate new information in LTM. Reviewing, cycling back, or referencing previously presented information that is linked to new information helps internalization. New associations and links to previous information help students firm up the previous information in their schema.

> **PRESENTATION PRINCIPLE—REDUNDANCY**
> Redundant information in an initial presentation can increase time to internalize.

Sensory Mode and Medium

Some information is better presented via a specific sensory mode, such as audio or visual information. For example, learning how to play a song on a guitar is likely better understood and internalized by a video and sound (or live demonstration) than text instructions. A sensory mode that is related to the nature of the learning outcome likely decreases time needed to internalize. Presenting supporting information in the same sensory mode as the outcome representation in LTM enhances internalization.

IPLT indicates that students learn some information better if the information is presented via multiple sensory modes (e.g., the multimedia principle of multimedia learning theory). This principle derives from the independence of visual and aural working memory. However, presenting redundant information via the same mode can hinder internalization; for example, presenting written text with a person reading the text aloud is less effective than images with spoken information and no text because text involves audio and visual processing (this is the redundancy principle of MML theory).

> **PRESENTATION PRINCIPLE—MULTIPLE SENSORY MODES**
> Using the appropriate sensory mode and/or multiple different modes can decrease time to internalize.

An information *medium* is the physical means of representing, transmitting, and storing information. Information stored or transmitted by a medium can include multiple sensory modes. A video recording, for example, uses dynamic images and spoken language to represent information. A textbook uses mainly text and static images. A telephone is a medium of aural information only.

Little empirical evidence supports the idea that medium alone affects internalization, though differences in media can affect the efficiency of presentation, including the cost of media and the time required to implement. Different media allow different levels of learner control of presentation. A book allows self-paced reading and review, a video clip allows review, and a lecture allows neither. The student control variable of media is one way media may matter for instruction.

Learner Control of Presentation

For enhancing internalization, a variable of media is the degree of control of presentation offered to the student by the medium. Some media allow students to control the speed at which information is presented (pacing and pausing). Other media allow information to be reviewed at the students' discretion (e.g., printed material). IPLT predicts that control of pacing will affect internalization because people vary in the speed in which they can process information.

Maintenance rehearsal, for example, is enhanced if a student can pause the presentation to rehearse presented information. Instructors should seek information presentation media that allow students to control aspects of presentation, particularly the speed of presentation. Preference for controllable presentation of information supports asynchronous presentation.

> **PRESENTATION PRINCIPLE—LEARNER CONTROL**
> Learner control of presentation pacing and review can reduce time to internalize.

Synchronicity of Presentation

Most current formal instructional environments, especially traditional classrooms, support a group-based model of instruction. Instructors guide the learning of a group of students in a single location (i.e., a classroom) within a specified time period. A one-size-fits-all approach is employed, where instructors present information targeted for the average student or struggling students.

Consequently, another variable of information presentation is whether information is presented in real time to the entire group (*synchronous presentation*) rather than to each student individually at a time and place of their choosing (*asynchronous presentation*). Presenting a worked-example on the whiteboard to a classroom of students is synchronous; having students watch a video as homework is asynchronous.

One advantage of asynchronous presentation is that presentation can be varied for each student based on learning variables of each individual student. With synchronous presentation, all students get the same presentation in the same way. With asynchronous presentation, students can choose when to attend to information and can review.

If attention wanders during synchronous presentation, students cannot review what they missed. Student attention is going to be distracted for many reasons during synchronous presentation, and they will miss some of the presented information. A potential advantage of synchronous presentation is spontaneity, which may appeal to some students.

> **PRESENTATION PRINCIPLE—SYNCHRONICITY**
> Matching synchronicity of presentation to learning objectives and student characteristics can improve internalization. Asynchronous presentation generally results in less time to internalize.

STUDENT VARIABLES OF INTERNALIZATION

Students vary in how well they internalize based on Carroll's variables of aptitude, prior knowledge, and motivation to pay attention. Do these student variables influence how information should be presented to individual students? In other words, do student differences affect how the above presentation variables affect internalization?

How instructors should alter information presentation based on differences in student attention, for example, is unclear. Though evidence is mixed, a reasonable hypothesis is that students with lower attention might benefit more from greater control of presentation. They can then review information they did not attended to. On the other hand, students with lower attention spans may be less able to judge how well they understand information presented at a specific pace.

Students also vary in learning ability, but whether different presentation methods differently affect the internalization of students with different learning ability has not been established despite decades of research in the area of aptitude-treatment interaction (ATI). Some evidence supports a principle that students with lower learning ability do less well when given more learner control, but the evidence is not strong and does not always support this principle.

It is unlikely that different presentation methods matter much for re-teaching remedial information that students need but lack. Little or no evidence suggests that remediation is more effective if specific instructional methods are used. Principles of quality information presentation are the same for students who need remediation and those who do not. Instructors, however, may seek to use more differentiated or individualized instruction for students who need remediation.

Characteristics of information presentation may also be differentially effective based on student prior knowledge. Previous knowledge, such as cultural expectations and norms, can affect how students attend to and interpret information and therefore matter for information selection. Using examples and terminology of a student's culture may be more effective because such information better matches the schemata of the students. However, a clear connection between prior knowledge (including cultural knowledge) and instructional presentation methods is not well established for learning performance.

In general, information presentation principles apply to all students regardless of student characteristics. The most important student variable that differentially affects information selection and presentation is prior student knowledge, which is addressed simply by additional instruction compatible with a cultural context (e.g., use of culturally relevant examples). Whether and how information presentation can be optimized to other student variables is a focus of continuing research.

TRADITIONAL PRESENTATION METHODS

Some presentation methods have been traditionally used for instruction in classrooms, such as lectures and textbooks. Traditional methods of information presentation have stood the test of time, but instructors may rely on such methods because of tradition rather than instructional design analysis.

Instructors have a schema for classroom instruction based on what they encountered as students. This schema may lead instructors to use traditional methods without evidence-based analysis. Text and lecturing have specific characteristics that may or may not be the ideal for presenting information for targeted internalization.

Lectures

Lecturing is strongly associated with instruction, but its ubiquity may be due more to the nature of the classroom environment than any advantages for internalization. Lecturing has some characteristics that should promote internalization, such as the ability to change based on student reaction. A lecture can change and adapt in real time based on how the instructor perceives students are attending.

Lecturing, being face-to-face, also uses all possible communication channels (e.g., gestures and intonation). The instructor's affect and attitudes are more easily discerned, leading to communication that is more comfortable to most students. Such social presence is thought by some to promote a better student-instructor relationship, which may affect attention and perseverance.

Lectures also have characteristics that may not promote internalization. Learners generally have no control of the content and pace of lectures. Information presented cannot be immediately reviewed. Lectures place students in the role of mainly passive listeners, which may lessen student attention. Lectures depend on the presentation skills of the instructor but also depend on the affect the lecturer presents to students.

A focus on relationships and instructor affect and attitude, plus the positive reaction of audiences to promotional and encouraging lectures, suggest that lectures are best for addressing affective and attitudinal learning objectives. These features may not be enough to compensate for the deficits of lecturing in terms of learner control and synchronicity for nonaffective cognitive objectives. The prescription is for instructors to use lecturing intentionally, not as a matter of habit or convenience.

Textbooks

Textbooks include primarily text supplemented with static images and diagrams. This traditional presentation medium is self-paced, can be asynchronous, and is often written at a level appropriate for grade level. These characteristics of textbooks make textbooks natural complements to lectures and can promote internalization.

The problem with textbooks is that reading requires more skill and effort than listening to a lecture or watching a video. Another issue with text is that the instructor does not determine the content. Though most textbooks are comprehensive and aligned with grade-level outcomes, they are often not designed to support internalization. Textbooks are designed to appeal to textbook selection committees and therefore tend to include too much information and seductive details that inhibit internalization. The only instructor control of content possible is to exclude parts of the text from student reading assignments.

The prescription for better internalization is for instructors to see textbooks as what they are—text-based information sources that often include irrelevant information designed to sell textbooks. All but the lowest-level courses should include text information sources, but the greatly increased access to information online means that instructors have more options for text material than they had in the past.

NEW PRESENTATION OPTIONS

The term "multimedia" has become common in education as classroom computers have replaced filmstrips, movies, and slides. The advent of digital media and internetworking of digital devices has resulted in new options for information presentation. Educational technology today provides alternatives for information presentation.

Computers offer easier access to dynamic media including audio and video. Computers also offer increased learner control of presentation including review and self-pacing. Additionally, computer-presented information allows hyperlinks among information, letting the student control how much information is presented or to find prerequisite and supplemental information.

Large-scale networking of digital devices (i.e., the Internet) allows students to access very large amounts of information on every topic imaginable. Unfortunately, there is no guarantee the information is accurate, which is why instructor guidance to online information is important. Access to other students is also greater due to online resources, increasing opportunities for peer collaboration.

Traditional information sources like textbooks can be used asynchronously, but digital media more strongly leads instructors to asynchronous presentation, placing more emphasis on students accessing information individually rather than the instructor presenting to a class. Digital media also lead instructors to use more asynchronous text-based peer discussion in the classroom.

Despite the opportunities offered by digital media, the new medium itself does not have learning benefits. It is the thoughtful selection of presentation characteristics offered by the new medium in light of learning principles that matters for improving instruction, not simply the use of newer media. Use of newer technology will have no benefits unless the presentation method is designed to optimally set variables identified in evidence-based learning principles.

Greater information presentation options place an increased burden on instructors for making decisions about information presentation. The principles listed in this chapter can help instructors make better choices about how information is presented based on characteristics of target outcomes and students.

SUMMING UP SUPPORTING INTERNALIZATION

The goal of this chapter is to get instructors to see internalization as a learning process supported primarily by instructor action to identify, select, and present information that promotes targeted internalization. Thoughtful design of information presentation can improve internalization, a necessary component to all academic learning.

Supporting internalization is not a matter of active learning, authentic context, twenty-first-century skills, or other commonly held ideas. Internalization is supported by judicious selection of information and optimizing how that information is presented based on variables mentioned in this chapter.

Although internalization is the focus of many learning theories, some educators demean internalization as passive or "instructor-centered" in comparison to active or "student-centered." This perspective plays down the vital role of internalization for all formal learning by ignoring that students must internalize sufficient new knowledge before they can learn from doing learning activities.

QUESTIONS

1. Someone other than the course instructor often selects at least some information sources. What information sources were selected for your course and who selected those sources? What factors did you consider before selecting the information you did choose?

2. How often do you lecture your classroom? (It may be instructive to keep a journal for a week of your classroom behavior.) What factors made you choose to lecture? What are some alternatives and why might those be better than lecturing?
3. A problem with asynchronous presentation is that the instructor cannot be sure the target information was presented to all students. How might an instructor take action to assure that students got the information?
4. What are some ways that instructors can attempt to increase student attention to presented information?
5. Given that many administrators stress "coverage" of all subtopics, how might instructors change the discussion to covering topics more slowly or in smaller units? (This is a good question for discussion with other instructors.)

REFERENCE

Rosenshine, B., and R. Stevens. "Teaching Functions." In *Handbook of Research on Teaching*, edited by M. C. Wittrock, 376–91. New York: MacMillan, 1986.

7

SUPPORTING EXTERNALIZATION

What this chapter is about: This chapter identifies potential variables that can affect student externalization for learning.
Why that matters: Externalization is an important learning process. Students that externalize knowledge learn much better than those who do not. Instructors need to know what might promote externalization.
Buzzwords relevant to this chapter: Hands-on learning, learning by doing, active learning.

Externalization is the process by which humans transform their knowledge into external information. People can express their knowledge in many ways, for example, with drawings or music. People can also express knowledge via a symbol system—as they do when they use language. An expression of information can be as simple as answering a question or as complex as writing a book.

Information people express is based on their knowledge, which is a unique network of personally generated associations. Humans cannot transmit to others their knowledge because telepathy is not among our current cognitive abilities. We must process our knowledge into information to express it. Information about our knowledge can be transmitted to others.

Language is a uniquely human means to express knowledge via symbolic information. Expression via language is commonplace in education. Learning objectives can, however, include nonsymbolic expressions such as created products or a performed skill. Students could be asked to create a sculpture or to demonstrate they can play the guitar.

Students must recall knowledge to externalize information. Retrieval of knowledge to working memory (WM) can result in reorganization of associations in long-term memory (LTM). In attempting to express information, students process their recalled knowledge. Such processing can change their knowledge (i.e., they learn). When students represent knowledge to help others understand, they reorganize their existing knowledge and generate new knowledge. Externalization results in learning that does not require presentation of new information.

SHOWER LEARNING

Have you noticed that you get insights or find solutions when taking a shower or driving a car? When people are in familiar and boring situations, their conscious minds wander and they begin to process their existing knowledge. Such processing can result in new insights and ideas.

Such shower processing shows that learning can occur merely from processing what is already known. Some educators call this process reflection. Refection is not externalization because reflection does not necessarily involve creation of externalized information. Additional processing beyond merely thinking is required to transform knowledge into external information.

Externalizing information is more effective than reflection for achieving learning objectives because instruction-guided expression is oriented to a task associated with target learning outcomes. Reflection is not necessarily on task with targeted learning. A reflection is also less likely to result in learning because it is more likely to confirm a student's current knowledge (including misconceptions).

> **EXTERNALIZATION PRINCIPLE**
> Learning activities that have students express their knowledge related to learning outcomes promote learning those outcomes.

COGNITIVE PROCESSES OF EXTERNALIZATION

The retrieval process of information processing learning theory (IPLT) is the transfer of knowledge from LTM to WM so the knowledge can be consciously processed to guide decisions and actions. Recalling information into working memory, however, is merely the first step in the externalization process. Working memory must further process the recalled knowledge into information to prepare it for transmission and reception by others.

IPLT and other learning theories focus on internalization rather than externalization. IPLT identifies and explains several control processes of internalization (as explained in chapter 4). Some of those control processes are likely involved with externalization (e.g., elaborative rehearsal, executive functions). Different control processes, however, are required to fully explain externalization, but no such processes are explicit in IPLT. The lack of theoretical modeling of externalization subprocesses means that the principles of externalization are not as well established as the principles of internalization.

Elaboration is an example of a cognitive process affecting externalization. Elaboration is a generative process involving the creation of new knowledge. People basically construct (i.e., make up) new information based on their existing knowledge. This process is a sort of the reverse of the elaborative rehearsal, the control process that involves the creation of new knowledge based on a merging of prior knowledge with new information. During retrieval, the new elaborated information is created from prior knowledge only.

MEMORY RECALL

A body of memory research has established some principles of the recall of memories that likely affect externalization. People recall knowledge based on cues from the environment that are associated with other knowledge via a schema. A specific stimulus can "activate" (make ready for processing in WM) a set of knowledge based on a schema in LTM. Many different bits of information (e.g., events and items) present during learning are associated in that schema.

Perception of a similar event or item recalls all associated information to working memory. This process is evident when, for example, people recall a past event or a specific location based on smelling a unique odor.

Students are better able to recall information when cues present during attempted recall are similar to those present at learning (this is called encoding specificity). This principle suggests that the instructor should assign externalization tasks that have cues similar to information presented during information presentation. Learning activities should be in similar contexts and situations as those used during internalization.

EXTERNALIZATION AND INSTRUCTION

Instruction that supports externalization promotes learning better than instruction for internalization only. For example, Roediger and Karpicke (2006) had students either read a section of text four times or read a section once and write down everything they could remember about it three times. The students were able to recall the sections they wrote about better than those they repeatedly read.

Instructors have long recognized the value of learning activities. Instructors assign learning activities, such as written products and worksheets, but also exams and quizzes. Having students answer questions is also a form of externalization. Good instructors seek to optimally set variables of learning activities to lessen time to learn or maximize the number of students who master learning objectives in a fixed time.

Because externalization primarily involves students processing their own knowledge, instructional support of externalization assumes that students already have some knowledge relevant to targeted learning. So some internalization must precede externalization. Given that internalization is also necessary for effective instruction, *a complete instructional method includes support for both internalization and externalization.*

LEARNING ACTIVITIES

Learning activities are tasks that instructors assign for students to express their knowledge in a way that supports learning objectives. Learning activities have students express their knowledge rather than the instructor presenting new information to students. Because different cognitive processes are involved with externalization, instructional support for learning assignments is different than support of internalization. Different learning variables are important for supporting externalization rather than internalization.

Some new information is often presented via a learning activity, so internalization and externalization may both be addressed, but each process requires different actions by the instructor to optimize learning. Using an activity to support internalization only can be done, but that type of activity would be guided by principles of information presentation rather than externalization principles.

Tests and quizzes are common externalizations. Jeffery Karpicke studied the effect of testing on learning and notes that "every time a person retrieves knowledge, that knowledge is changed, because retrieving knowledge improves one's ability to retrieve it again in the future. Practicing retrieval does not merely produce rote, transient learning; it produces meaningful, long-term learning" (2012, 157). Evidence indicates that testing improves learning more than spending equal time intentionally studying the content.

Other externalizations include typical homework tasks including worksheets, written documents, physical models, and presentations. Learning activities are also used to address higher-order learning outcomes such as application of knowledge to solve problems or generation of new information.

VARIABLES THAT AFFECT SELECTION OF LEARNING ACTIVITIES

How to choose externalization tasks that support specific learning outcomes is a major instructional design issue. Characteristics of instruction that promote externalization and elaboration of existing knowledge are not well known, so prescribing support for externalization is more speculative that prescribing support for internalization. However, some principles from IPLT and other learning theories can guide the design and selection of learning activities based on the following variables.

Prior Knowledge (i.e., Meaningfulness)

Because externalization depends on existing student knowledge, exactly what prior knowledge a student has is very important for determining effective learning activities. Students must have sufficient knowledge for productive processing in doing a learning activity.

Students' prior knowledge could be the result of previous learning, but more often the knowledge is the result of recent instruction that presented information in support of the learning outcome that is the target of the activity. It is recommended that instructors assess students' prior knowledge related to learning activities even if the information was presented previously or if the information is presented as part of the assignment.

Type of Learning Outcome Use

The *transfer appropriate processing principle* states that better learning occurs when the encoding process better matches the retrieval process. Students can better retrieve knowledge via a process that is similar to the process used to learn the knowledge. The *levels-of-processing principle* states that processing based on meaning usually results in better learning. These principles apply to externalization, suggesting that some types of tasks better promote the learning of specific *types* of outcomes.

Useful learning outcomes include both a *type* and *expected use* of knowledge. Both the knowledge type and use should guide specification of a learning activity, but the expected use of a targeted learning outcome is the strongest indicator of appropriate learning activities. Activities that have students use their knowledge as specified in the learning outcome better support targeted learning.

For example, a task that requires students to classify items into general or new categories (not presented in instruction) likely supports a learning outcome involving concept formation. Having students answer questions on a quiz is an appropriate activity for recall of facts. Instruction that targets procedures as learning outcomes can involve multiple knowledge uses including stating the procedure, applying the procedure in specific contexts, applying the procedure in new (untaught) contexts, or finding a new procedure.

Higher-order outcomes also involve multiple enabling outcomes. Using knowledge to solve a specific problem involves more than recall, such as identifying whether the solution is appropriate for a given problem. Research shows that students *generate* new knowledge better with some guidance. In some cases, synthesis of new ideas may be the targeted learning outcome and thus the learning activity should have students attempt a creation task, but only after guidance is provided about how one might do so.

Instructors should avoid the mistake of assuming that assigning higher-order learning tasks will automatically result in higher-order learning. Asking students to do an activity does not mean they will successfully do so. When asked to create new knowledge, many students will fail to produce any valid knowledge that aligns with target learning outcomes and often will simply reinforce their own misconceptions.

Learning activities that require higher-order use of knowledge are not guaranteed to result in higher-order learning. Also, stating a mostly unachievable learning objective does not make that outcome more likely to be achieved by students. Instructor expectation is not an effective learning method. One often hears that increased expectations will lead to improved learning, but higher expectations alone are unlikely to improve performance unless accompanied by appropriate instruction.

> **EXTERNALIZATION PRINCIPLE—USE ALIGNMENT**
> Learning activities should have students use targeted types of knowledge as specified by target learning outcomes.

Authenticity

Learning activities that have students use knowledge in a context that is similar to the context of expected performance are deemed "authentic." This label is especially appropriate if the context is part of the "real world," meaning other than typical classroom contexts. Learning performance is highly contextual, so better learning activities should mimic the expected context of performance. More authentic activities result in improved learning performance in that context because it provides more cues that help students recall relevant knowledge.

The concept of a schema of knowledge supports an emphasis on context of use. The goal of instruction is to create, change, or expand schema, and the more that schema reflects the environment of use, the more effective the schema will be for supporting targeted use of knowledge in that specific context.

Unfortunately, determining exactly what makes a context or activity authentic is not always obvious or straightforward. The recommendation of authentic activities may promise more than it can deliver. Many learning outcomes have general application and therefore can be associated with many different contexts.

Many academic goals are authentic in an academic context, such as determining the main theme of a story. The common example of applying math in some application such as carpentry is a context that most math learners will never encounter. How students will eventually need to use their knowledge is hard to predict.

Advocating authenticity is easy; finding activities with generality to "real-world" contexts, however that is defined, is more difficult. In fact, authentic instruction may merely involve proper selection of the type of use of target learning outcomes. Assigning "real-world" activities provides no learning benefits unless the activities are very common or the activity is general enough to apply in many contexts, but such generality is the opposite of authenticity.

> **EXTERNALIZATION PRINCIPLE—AUTHENTICITY**
> Using learning activities with contexts similar to that in which performance is expected improves performance in that context.

Feedback

Feedback is a comment, assessment, or evaluation about a student expression made by an instructor or peer. Generally, some feedback of an externalization is accepted as superior to no feedback because feedback provides new information that helps students further process their expressed knowledge.

Different types of feedback can be given, such as simple correct/incorrect judgments, stating correct or preferred responses, or explanation about why the response is satisfactory or not. How different feedback affects learning is an open question, with a growing body of research. Generally, feedback that provides more information is considered superior for supporting targeted learning.

Again, the idea that feedback is useful in helping students learn from learning activities is not new to instructors. Feedback has long been recognized as an important guidance support for learning. Instructors can improve the quality of their instruction by providing feedback of an appropriate type for the targeted outcome. Generally, more feedback is better, but providing feedback is very labor intensive and instructors often lack sufficient time and resources to provide high levels of feedback tailored to individual students.

> **EXTERNALIZATION PRINCIPLE—FEEDBACK**
> Providing feedback about a student's externalization improves targeted processing for achievement of target outcomes.

Instructional Guidance/Learner Control

Learning activities inherently offer some degree of learner control because they give students some leeway in how they respond. Externalization is based on what a learner knows, and how a student responds to an instructional task is up to the student. Instructor guidance is mainly determined by selection of the learning activity, instructions that accompany the activity, and feedback provided.

Examples of increased guidance (less learner control) include discussion scripts that direct students to follow an explicit procedure during discussion. Having students write a paper can include a "rubric" that specifies in detail what information should be included in the paper. Exams and quizzes exhibit high instructor control, but instructors can use more open-ended questions or let students select which questions they answer.

Some categories of knowledge use, such as "find" or "generate," are likely better supported by activities that require higher degrees of learner control. An activity requiring recall of definitions likely allows little student variation in response. Applying a principle generally likely involves more learner discretion, finding a principle even more. To improve participation and persistence through more student choice, instructors can offer multiple equally appropriate activities for students to select from.

Whether higher learner control within the activity promotes better externalization is an open question. Granting students control of creating a learning activity is risky because students lack knowledge about how to select supportive activities. Students, for example, lack a clear understanding of what tasks are appropriate for specific learning objectives. What is clear is that some learning objectives, particularly generative and creative objectives, require greater learner control of the learning activity for students to practice the targeted objective.

> **EXTERNALIZATION PRINCIPLE—LEARNER CONTROL**
>
> The knowledge use specified in targeted learning outcomes suggests how much learner control is beneficial for that outcome.

Conceptual Conflict

Learning tasks are more effective when they have students compare their knowledge to alternatives. Consideration of alternatives by expression of prior knowledge is difficult because alternatives (and supporting evidence) are not always part of a student's existing knowledge. Learning tasks that promote consideration of alternatives often involve conceptual conflict—alternatives that conflict with students' existing beliefs.

Activities intended to promote conceptual change likely require stronger instructor guidance. Conceptual conflict is unlikely to occur unless students are explicitly directed to consider alternatives. And consideration of alternatives likely requires presentation or access to new information—the alternatives and associated supporting evidence. New information can come from the instructor, or finding such information can be part of the activity.

Recall that achieving conceptual change is more difficult than adding new knowledge. Supporting conceptual change always involves conceptual conflict because new information conflicts with knowledge that is to be changed. Presenting conflicting information alone rarely is sufficient to change well-established concepts. Learning activities that lead students to process the new information and reflect on their current beliefs have a better chance of initiating conceptual change, though the goal is difficult to achieve even with very good learning activities that make students confront contradictions.

An example of an instructional method that promotes consideration of alternatives is the structured academic controversy (SAC). This method formalizes a process of taking different perspectives that helps students use critical thinking to resolve conceptual conflict.

> **EXTERNALIZATION PRINCIPLE—CONCEPTUAL CONFLICT**
> Activities that promote comparison of personal knowledge/belief to alternatives promote cognitive processing for conceptual change.

LEARNING BY DOING

Learning by doing, also called hands-on or active learning, is instruction based primarily on assigning learning activities and de-emphasizing classroom lecturing. Learning by doing is often asserted as superior to so-called passive learning. This perspective tends to pit externalization against internalization, which is a false dichotomy because more effective instruction requires support of both processes.

If the learning goal is to have students state facts, learn concept definitions, or solve specific problems, then doing may not be as effective as telling. Sweller and Cooper (1985) found that having students try to solve problems and find solutions on their own is less effective and efficient than showing them how to solve the problems (i.e., showing worked examples—a presentation of information). Even students who found solutions on their own did not perform as well as those who were shown worked examples.

Learning by doing activities can fail if the activities do not involve processing to support targeted learning outcomes. Most instructors seek to have students learn more than targeted objectives, but instructors must be careful that additional activities and information do not distract from targeted goals. Limitations of attention and working memory capacity, in addition to limitations on instructional time, mean that more is not necessarily better.

Learning by doing is learning via externalization and thus is a very important aspect of instruction. However, instruction by doing alone is not effective without effective presentation of information to support the doing. High-quality instruction attempts to optimize both internalization and externalization by coordinating presentation with activity to achieve the quickest time to learn for the highest number of students.

TESTING FOR ASSESSMENT OR LEARNING

Educational assessment can have multiple different goals. One goal is to provide overall performance feedback to students. Another is to help instructors adjust their instruction to be more effective. Assessment is also done to compare relative performance of schools and districts to provide information to educational decision makers. Several principles for valid and reliable assessment of learning can be found from many sources (e.g., Phye 1997).

Tests also can be given to promote learning. For that purpose, instructors create exams and quizzes as learning activities. Such tests should be designed based on the principles for learning activities, not assessments.

Because tests are externalizations, they can provide the same learning benefits as learning activities. All activities in which students express their knowledge can have learning benefits of externalization, regardless of their intended use. The effectiveness of an activity is, however, improved if it is designed with the intended purpose clearly in mind. What distinguishes an activity as a learning activity rather than an assessment is merely the intended purpose of the activity.

QUESTIONING

An easy and very common externalization task is answering a question. Questions can be used in many ways, for example, to review and support presented information, to check student understanding, to identify misconceptions, or to provide an answer or summary that is in a form more understandable by other students.

Questions have several relevant variables. The expected answers of questions, of course, should relate to the type and use of the targeted learning outcome. Expected answers can be products or processes. Openness is the degree to which alternative answers are accepted as valid. Probing questions are follow-up questions based on a specific student answer.

Questioning can be done during information presentation to support internalization. Such questioning checks audience understanding but also leads the audience to further processing of presented information. Use of questioning during a lecture transforms the lecture into a lecture-discussion, which, unlike a lecture, is a complete instructional method that may suffice for some learning goals. Instructors who present information largely via speaking in real time should include frequent questioning in their presentations.

Testing for Learning

Research supports the use of quizzes to support learning. Frequent and short testing has learning benefits for most types of outcomes. Even selected-response exams, with minimal feedback, result in better learning performance than no testing or extended study time. This idea is contrary to assertions of too much testing in formal education, though it should be clear that the type and goal of testing matter for evaluating whether too much testing is being done. For example, quizzing for learning is ideally done frequently and shortly after information presentation.

High-stakes standardized tests are not delivered a short time after information presentation. Such tests address general knowledge (many learning outcomes) instead of focusing on recent instruction. So standardized testing done long after instruction is not as conducive to learning as quizzes or exams that occur shortly after instruction and test more specific learning objectives.

> **EXTERNALIZATION PRINCIPLE—TESTING FOR LEARNING**
> Tasks involving recall via constructed externalization are more beneficial than tasks involving identification. Frequent on-topic testing is beneficial for learning.

Generally speaking, variables affecting learning activities also affect the use of tests for learning. Some variables, however, are of more interest for tests. Learner control of testing, as with other learning activities, can benefit from reviewability and self-pacing but includes some additional caveats. *Self-assessment*, for example, can be useful for learning, but instructors should keep in mind that research has shown that people are generally poor self-assessors.

Self-assessment should provide clear guidance about how students should assess their performance (i.e., based on what aspects of their responses). Letting students evaluate themselves based on their own judgment of correct responses or quality performance is dangerous because students are more likely to reach faulty conclusions about their own performance.

For improved learning or assessment, a clear goal is required. If the goal is to support instructional decisions (e.g., whether to present remedial instruction), assessment design should focus on reliably identifying student prior knowledge or achievement of learning objectives. If the goal is to improve learning, the emphasis is on whether the task appropriately stimulates externalization that supports learning objectives. These goals are not incompatible—an assessment can do both—but better assessments can result from clear identification of instructional goals and intentional design.

EXTERNALIZATION SUMMARY

Karpicke stresses that retrieval must be part of analysis of learning:

Basic research on learning and memory . . . has emphasized that retrieval must be considered in any analysis of learning. In part, this is because people do not store static, exact copies of experiences that are reproduced verbatim at retrieval. Instead, knowledge is actively reconstructed on the basis of the present context and available retrieval cues. (2012, 158)

Such reconstruction based on current context is very important for long-term use of knowledge and the creation of new (i.e., deeper) knowledge related to retrieved knowledge. Instructors use retrieval to support learning by providing tasks (e.g., worksheets, papers, and projects) in which students externalize their current knowledge via learning activities designed in regard to the type of knowledge and use of knowledge specified by targeted learning outcomes.

QUESTIONS

1. Pick one of your current instructional units and assess the learning activities in terms of the learning variables listed in this chapter. If you are not an instructor, what ways have instructors had you externalize as a student?
2. In your opinion, how often do you lecture your classroom? What factors made you choose to lecture? What are some alternatives and why might those be better than lecturing?
3. A problem with asynchronous presentation is that the instructor cannot be sure the target information was presented to all students. How might an instructor take action to assure that students got the information?
4. What are some ways that instructors can attempt to increase student attention to presented information?
5. Given that many administrators stress "coverage" of all subtopics, how might instructors change the discussion to covering topics more slowly or in smaller units? (This is a good question for discussion with other instructors.)

REFERENCES

Karpicke, Jeffery. D. "Retrieval-Based Learning: Active Retrieval Promotes Meaningful Learning." *Current Directions in Psychological Science* 21, no. 3 (2012): 157–63.

Phye, Gary D. *Handbook of Classroom Assessment: Learning, Achievement, and Adjustment.* San Diego: Academic Press, 1997.

Roediger, Henry L., and Jeffrey D. Karpicke. "The Power of Testing Memory." *Perspectives on Psychological Science* 1, no. 3 (Sept. 2006): 181–210.

Sweller, John, and Graham A. Cooper. "The Use of Worked Examples as a Substitute for Problem Solving in Learning Algebra." *Cognition and Instruction* 2, no. 1 (1985): 59–89.

8

INSTRUCTIONAL ENVIRONMENTS

What this chapter is about: This chapter discusses the distinguishing characteristics of online versus classroom instructional environments and the significance of such differences for instructional effectiveness.
Why that matters: The online environment is being increasingly used for all types of instruction. Instructors need to know the learning ramifications of this change in instructional environments.
Buzzwords relevant to this chapter: MOOCs, flipped classrooms, online learning, e-learning.

An instructional environment is the set of environmental conditions under which instruction occurs. The two most commonly used instructional environments are classroom and online. With the traditional classroom environment, instruction takes place in a classroom at a specific time and with an instructor and students interacting face-to-face.

The online environment does not have students gather at a specific place and time and so requires that all interaction be mediated. Interaction occurs via networked digital devices that provide audio, video, and text communication.

The two instructional environments differ in which learning variables are fixed by the environment. For example, face-to-face instruction is not a variable that an instructional designer can control using online instruction.

The classroom and online environments are not very different in what is instructionally possible. Despite the lack of face-to-face interaction, the online environment supports a wide variety of communication modes and therefore can support almost all instructional methods that are available in the classroom environment. Most instructional methods can be employed in both environments, and research generally supports equal instructional effectiveness.

Each environment, however, favors specific instructional methods because some methods are easier to implement within the environment. Differences in ease of setting learning variables in each environment result in different instructional methods typically used in each environment. For example, the online environment tends to favor asynchronous discussion (that does not occur simultaneously in real time) and classrooms favor synchronous discussion. Both types of discussion are possible in each environment, but the amount of effort required to implement each type varies.

The U.S. DOE report on online learning by Means and colleagues (2009) recognizes that differences in instructional effectiveness of the two environments likely result from differences in instructional methods used in each environment:

> Findings of this meta-analysis should not be construed as demonstrating that online learning is superior as a medium. Rather, it is the combination of elements in the treatment conditions, which are likely to include additional learning time and materials as well as additional opportunities for collaboration, that has proven effective. (51)

The online environment has some advantages in terms of accessibility and cost of instruction. No physical plant is necessary beyond students and instructor having proper digital devices, potentially resulting in huge cost savings. No room or building that must be heated and lighted is required. No devices are needed for multimedia presentation. No paper is used for assignments. Online classes also have potential economic benefits in terms of how many students can be instructed by a single instructor.

FAVORED METHODS OF ONLINE VERSUS CLASSROOM

The online environment, by definition, does not support the information presentation mode most promoted by the classroom environment:

face-to-face oral presentation. Therefore, online and classroom instructional designs tend to differ mostly in the way information is presented, especially the synchronicity of presented information.

Online Versus Classroom Information Presentation

Online tends to give students more control because asynchronous mediated presentations let students choose when to attend to the presentation. Use of recorded media and text also allows students more control over the pace and review of the information. The propensity of online instruction to employ asynchronous mediated information presentation methods can account for the greater effectiveness found in some comparisons of online versus classroom performance.

Online Versus Classroom Learning Activities

The two instructional environments tend to differ little in type of learning activities used. Synchronous learning activities tend to be used more in classrooms, such as in-class worksheets, lab experiments, and so on. Synchronous activities are more difficult to implement online. Traditional classrooms, however, have long used homework, papers, and projects that are done asynchronously.

Traditional classrooms include "seatwork," simultaneous activities, and labs that make use of the physical classroom environments. These are unavailable online except via simulation, limiting the "hands-on" ability of online courses, which must rely on simulation of hands-on activities.

HYBRID ENVIRONMENTS

Hybrid or "blended" environments are classrooms with scheduled meeting times but also with access to online information and activities via networked digital devices. The asynchronous methods that tend to be used online can be implemented in hybrid courses in addition to face-to-face presentation and hands-on activities.

Internet support in classrooms has resulted in the idea of "flipping" courses. Flipped courses intend to reduce lecturing and increase learning activities (including discussion) during class meeting time. Advocates of flipping assert that these changes result from simply presenting lectures asynchronously online prior to class.

Flipping does result in changes in instruction, but it retains lectures as the prime means of information presentation. Unfortunately, recorded lectures eliminate the features that make lectures potentially attractive as presentation methods (i.e., social presence, spontaneity, ability to react). Teachers also cannot be sure that students watched the lecture before class. The effort to better use class time for "doing" results in more reliance on poorer-quality lecturing for presentation.

Big gains in instructional effectiveness cannot be expected from flipping beyond getting instructors to use less class time primarily to present information. Less time presenting results in more class time doing learning activities, which can show differences in learning performance. Classroom environments, however, have always supported a flipped method by assigning textbook or other reading assignments prior to class.

Many classroom instructors have already implemented instructional strategies that rely more on classroom learning activities without flipping. Any improvements in learning performance are likely due to increased support of learning activities rather than making lectures asynchronous.

INSTRUCTOR RESPONSE TO INSTRUCTIONAL ENVIRONMENTS

Instructors should intentionally select presentation and learning activities based on instructional principles, not based on effort to implement or what has been traditionally done within the environment. Classroom designers must decide how to use the synchronous nature of classrooms to best effect. Online designers must focus on ways to compensate for the lack of actual personal contact between instructor and students and among students.

Networked digital technology presents an opportunity to break classroom reliance on instructor lecturing and the synchronicity prominent in instruction in the classroom. But such changes are better done based on analysis and design rather than simply doing what comes easy within an instructional environment or what others have typically done.

The ratio of the number of students to instructors is another characteristic distinguishing the two instructional environments. The traditional classroom environment supports a rather high ratio of about twenty to forty students to one instructor, though the ratio is often smaller for specific groups such as special education and elementary students. This high ratio is the result of practical and economic limitations and is contrary to evidence that smaller ratios better support learning.

The ratio of 1 to 1, sometimes called "tutoring," has been proposed as the most effective ratio (instruction is completely individualized to the student). Modern methods, such as the multi-tiered system of support (MTSS), allow high ratios of student-to-teacher during initial instruction, but provide lower ratios for remedial instruction for students who do not achieve targeted learning performance via initial instruction.

Student-to-teacher ratios are more fluid in the online environment because even higher ratios can be supported. An extreme example is the massive open online courses (MOOCs) in which thousands of students can be "taught" by one instructor. MOOCs use specific types of instructional methods often involving lecturing and peer interaction. MOOCs mediate lectures and put them online, where they become information sources for sometimes thousands of students.

This approach, like flipping, eliminates some of the effective features of lectures by mediating them. The idea seems to be that the quality of lecturing of "star" professors is more effective for achieving learning outcomes, a dubious assertion regardless of the quality of the information presented in the lecture.

Externalizations in MOOCs are done asynchronously and tend to rely on peer interaction for feedback and evaluation. The instructor does not interact with student externalizations or assessment and therefore is not part of the instructional method beyond lecturing and specification of learning activities. MOOCs are likely to be effective mainly for students with high self-motivation and self-regulation with the ability to learn on their own given good information rather than any merit of the environment itself.

The de-emphasis of lecturing and synchronous activities of the online environment likely means that higher instructor-to-student ratios are better supported online, but the effect of higher ratios in the online environment is an open research question. The available effort of instructors in online courses may be better used to provide more interaction with a smaller number of students than supporting more students at lower levels of feedback and interaction.

SUMMARY

The bottom line is that instructional method matters more than instructional environments. That said, it must be recognized that the classroom and online environments, though capable of supporting many instructional methods, lead instructors to some methods over others.

Online instructional methods tend to de-emphasize lectures for information presentation and use more asynchronous presentation and assignment of learning activities. Effective choices for instructional methods, based on evidence-based principles, are the goal for improved instructional quality regardless of the instructional environment. Instructors should resist letting the instructional environment determine instructional methods without due consideration of the appropriateness of the method for students and learning goals.

The instructional environment itself is unlikely to have a major effect on learning. Research tends to show little or no difference for instruction in either environment if similar instructional methods are used. Assertions that online instruction will improve student performance are questionable, though benefits in convenience and cost may be realized with the online environment.

QUESTIONS

1. If you currently use online resources, reflect on how you use them to present information, deal with learning assignments, or manage instruction. If you do not, think about how you could use online resources.

2. Given that online and classroom environments differ mainly on synchronicity of presentation and assignments, what problems can be expected from moving a classroom course to an online course?
3. Which learning environment is more effective: classroom, online, or hybrid? Why do you think so?
4. Can instructional environments be compared for effectiveness given that they tend to employ different instructional methods? Why or why not?

REFERENCE

Means, B., Y. Toyama, R. Murphy, M. Bakia, and K. Jones. *Evaluation of Evidence Based Practices in Online Learning: A Meta Analysis and Review of Online Learning Studies*. Washington, DC: U.S. Department of Education Office of Planning Evaluation and Policy Development, 2009.

9

PEER-TO-PEER COLLABORATIVE LEARNING METHODS

What this chapter is about: This chapter reviews the learning and instructional principles associated with collaborative instructional methods.

Why that matters: Group-based instruction has been increasingly implemented in all instructional settings. Understanding why peer collaboration is effective, and which variables influence its effectiveness, is increasingly important for instructors to know.

Many educators and researchers have focused on the effect of direct interpersonal communication on learning. Humans seem particularly affected by information coming directly from another human, especially if that human is a trusted family member, friend, teacher, or peer. Humans have likely evolved to have a preference to learn from others, which is suggested by the long childhood of humans compared to other animals. Humans are designed to learn from other humans. Such focus has led to emphasis on social interaction in human instruction, including recent emphasis on social-emotional learning, emotional intelligence, and peer-to-peer learning.

Humans naturally are primed to mimic behavior they observe in others. So humans are good observational learners and also tend to do what other humans tell them to do. These characteristics make human interaction a powerful learning mechanism and also show the importance of instructional guidance.

Collaborative "learning" is an instructional strategy in which students present information to each other and do learning activities in small groups. The strong evidence of the effectiveness of collaborative methods has resulted in increased use of collaborative methods at all levels of formal instruction.

Collaborative methods involve potential learning variables that are different than methods intended for individual students and thus warrant further discussion about how collaborative methods should be optimized for effectiveness. It is important for instructors to understand that peer learning is not simply more knowledgeable students teaching less knowledgeable ones (as suggested by Vygotsky). Research has established that peers with equal knowledge can help each other learn things that neither can learn alone.

All collaborative learning methods involve small groups of students (as small as two) addressing a task usually determined by the instructor. Interaction with the instructor is minimized, though the instructor has the responsibility for keeping discussion on track for meeting learning objectives.

From an I-E instructional model perspective, collaborative methods use peer interactions to present new information and also support expression of knowledge with and to other group members. Such methods combine information presentation from students with expression to other students. One student's expression is an information source for other students.

How collaborative learning works is not clearly established by learning theory. Because students have similar knowledge about targeted learning, they are more likely to understand information expressed by peers than from instructors or experts. Paradoxically, differences in peer understanding also promote learning by providing diverse information that causes conceptual conflict that a lone student cannot achieve through externalization. In addition, expressing to peers is more likely to get students to process information to help others understand, thereby deepening their own knowledge. These factors are responsible for the effectiveness of collaborative methods.

Such ideas about how peer-to-peer instruction works suggest that the prior knowledge of students and their ability to express that knowledge are important factors affecting collaborative learning. The similarity and difference in the prior knowledge of group members is therefore an important variable. Additionally, the need for students to interact and communicate is vital to the success of collaborative learning. The amount of interaction is related to the effectiveness of this instruction strategy.

Another important variable of collaborative learning methods is goal structure. Goal structure determines how success is defined for a learning activity. If student activity is evaluated based on how individual performance compares to others, the goal structure is competitive. An example is grading on a curve or giving only a specific percentage of each letter grade (i.e., A, B, C, etc.). Individualistic goal structures reward students based only on stated criteria; everybody can earn an A. The performance of others is unrelated to individual performance.

A cooperative goal structure relates an individual's evaluation to level of effort of the group. Thus, each group member is aware that the success of the group will affect their individual evaluation. Students feel dependent on the efforts of other students. Only when this goal structure is implemented is the method truly collaborative for learning. This structure implies that a measure of group interdependence is a means to measure and evaluate the quality of a collaborative method.

In general, collaborative learning activities should be selected based on the same principles that guide selection of individual learning activities. A key variable is the intended use stated in the targeted learning outcomes. Tasks that involve classification are good for addressing understanding concepts. Tasks having students recall and apply procedures promote student achievement of application of procedural knowledge. Tasks requiring generation or synthesis may promote achievement of outcomes involving creation.

Two types of collaborative methods often used by instructors are peer discussion and reciprocal teaching. Principles supporting these methods are the subject of current research, but some guidance can be provided to instructors for improving effectiveness.

PEER DISCUSSION FOR LEARNING

Peer discussion is a method that has students primarily communicate with each other to address a learning task. Peer discussion is used both in classrooms and online, though online discussion tends to be asynchronous and text-based and classroom discussion tends to be synchronous speech, though either environment can support both.

Selection of Discussion Tasks

Instructors choose peer discussion tasks based on the same principles used for choosing other learning activities. Tasks can have different goals such as solving a problem, presenting an argument, finding an answer, producing a product, and so forth. Tasks often are simply a position taken on an issue or question, a verbal expression of group consensus. Merely asking students to discuss a topic (i.e., without a clear goal) is not a valid instructional task.

Discussion tasks likely stimulate more potentially productive discussion if the task promotes conceptual conflict within the group. Controversial topics associated with discussion tasks are more likely to result in increased conceptual conflict for sufficient group processing. This quality of discussion depends on expressed differences among students. This leads to a collaborative instructional principle that diverse groups are better than homogeneous groups.

Discussion Procedure

Instructors explicitly direct the discussion process. How students interact can be quite open and undefined or can be restricted and guided. Scripts, for example, can guide how students respond to the discussion task. An instructor can require that students conform to a discussion format that includes assertion and supporting evidence. Instructors can require students to classify their responses (i.e., "evidence" versus "opinion") by labeling each response. By making groups produce all necessary elements of a formal argument, higher-quality discussion that targets logical thinking can be realized.

Scripting discussion often guides the type of processing done and gets students to process information in ways they might not do without scripts. On the other hand, scripting may reduce divergent responses. This dilemma is simply another example that effective instructional guidance is not rigid but flexibly based on targeted outcomes, student variables, and characteristics of the environment. If the target outcome involves creating better arguments to support assertions, then more guidance about how to make good arguments is likely to have better results than more open responses.

An example of a more rigidly guided interaction is the structured academic controversy (SAC) that requires students to examine a controversial topic from both (or all) sides. Students must follow the format of the SAC in discussing the topic. The SAC has groups argue with other groups, and then the groups change sides and argue from the other perspective. Evidence suggests that SAC is effective in bringing about conceptual change.

Discussion Participation

Students cannot learn from discussion, or any learning activity, unless they participate. A clear principle of discussion for learning is that greater participation in the discussion results in better learning. Indeed, participation in the discussion is more important than the quality of the group expressions.

Getting adequate participation from all students is difficult. Instructional efforts to promote participation include making participation important for students' course grades or requiring a minimum number of contributions from each group member, which is easy to track online where responses are recorded.

To effectively use peer discussion, some instructional effort must be made to encourage participation. All peer discussion methods should include a strategy to increase and maintain participation.

Quality of Discussion

Participation alone does not ensure optimum probability of achieving learning goals within the allotted discussion time. Students must adequately process information by discussion to promote learning (e.g., see Jorczak and Bart 2009).

Students often seek to minimize time and effort in discussion by agreeing on an answer as quickly as possible. Alternatively, students think they only have to express their opinions and beliefs to adequately contribute to the discussion. In fact, such rush to agreement and stating of opinions often results in no learning and results in some educators having a low opinion of peer discussion for learning. Discussion must display specific characteristics, including high participation, to support learning.

Deeper discussion for learning occurs when students disagree by expressing *divergent information*. Divergent information increases cognitive conflict that the group must process in trying to come to a consensus. Students who work to resolve disagreement more fully consider alternatives and reanalyze their initial opinions (see, for example, a study by Kanuka [2006]). Instructors can contribute to the discussion by encouraging conflict by asking questions or even arguing against the position of the group if that position did not result from adequate consideration of alternatives.

Generally, a productive discussion results from students at first expressing sufficient divergent information that leads to more group processing and then leads to a convergence of information to a common group response (see Jorczak 2011). Having groups share their responses with the other groups in the class results in more diversity of information and expression that promotes learning.

> **DISCUSSION PRINCIPLE—DIVERGENCE AND CONVERGENCE**
> Information presented in discussion that first diverges and then converges on group consensus better promotes learning.

Synchronicity and Medium of Discussion

Discussion among students can occur via spoken language in real time or via a medium that allows discussion to occur asynchronously. Face-to-face synchronous communication has the advantage that all communication modes can be employed (like body language and voice inflection). Face-to-face communication is said to provide more social presence, which is the feeling of social and emotional closeness a student feels when they are communicating with another student. Research to date, however, has been unable to establish that lack of communication modes negatively affects learning performance.

Synchronous oral discussion is more appropriate for younger (or struggling) students who are still learning to write. Younger students also respond better to the positive feelings humans have in communicating face-to-face.

Mediated communication excludes communication modes, often requiring more effort by students to express their knowledge. Asynchronous communication has the advantage of letting students respond at their own pace and allows much more time to process other students' messages and their own responses.

Asynchronous communication gives students as much time as they need to attend to information, compose an externalization, and review and edit what they say. Everyone has the opportunity to say all they want; nobody can dominate the conversation to the exclusion of others. Writing messages offers some benefits of increased organization and cognitive processing compared to face-to-face conversation.

> **DISCUSSION PRINCIPLE—SYNCHRONICITY**
> Synchronous spoken discussion is easier and more satisfying to most students. Asynchronous text-based discussion better promotes processing for learning.

The use of peer collaboration for learning is sometimes labeled "learner centered" (or "student centered") as opposed to "teacher centered." The label "centered," however, is a misnomer and a buzzword. All instruction is centered on achieving targeted student learning. This issue is not centering, whatever that means, but rather how important learning variables, such as goal structure, synchronicity, and group diversity, are set.

Cognitive information processing principles explain why collaborative discussion works so well. The learning variables involved in making discussion effective include how well information presented by peers is understood and the depth of processing required for collaboration. The amount of divergence present in a discussion is a variable that affects depth of processing.

RECIPROCAL TEACHING

While collaborative learning activities always include some discussion among group members, not all collaborative learning activities focus on discussion results. Many collaborative tasks result in products (as when a group produces a slide show) rather than the group reaching a discussion consensus. Large projects for groups include multiple component activities that promote externalization for learning.

Reciprocal teaching is a collaborative learning method in which group members take turns teaching (presenting) each other some of the content (information) supportive of targeted learning. Each group member, in turn, assumes the roll of instructor for the rest of the group.

This method is effective because the task guides students to process information to promote knowledge construction in peers. The method promotes externalization in the teacher and promotes internalization in the listeners because information is presented at the level and uses terminology of the learners. The teacher tends to focus on points that help him or her understand the information, and the other students are likely to have similar needs.

The course instructor supports reciprocal teaching by identifying what should be taught and learned, the target learning outcomes of the reciprocal teaching activity, and monitoring the groups. In practice, many instructors have noticed that attempting to teach others is an extremely effective externalization for the teacher. Research has generally supported this conclusion. The processing required to externalize information thought to be effective for teaching others is particularly effective in promoting reorganization of knowledge.

Being able to teach a concept, procedure, and so on is likely to be designated as a learning outcome. The knowledge use "to teach" is rarely found in learning outcomes, but that use of knowledge is very effective for achieving many learning outcomes. Knowledge use for teaching should be considered for student activities even though it is not listed as a use of knowledge in learning taxonomies or target learning outcomes.

COLLABORATIVE METHODS SUMMARY

Collaborative instructional activities are effective because they merge internalization and externalization of peers, who are more likely to present and process information at the level of their understanding. Instructors have near-expert knowledge of the subject and cannot always communicate at a level optimal for student understanding. Collaboration also works because each member of the group feels a responsibility to the group to put forth effort to learn (ideally). Collaborative activities should be chosen on the same basis as individual learning activities but also have additional considerations.

QUESTIONS

1. Select a learning activity designed for individual students and convert it a collaborative activity for small groups. Characterize the changes that were required.
2. Select at random a couple of standards (or learning objectives) for a course you have taught or seek to teach. Brainstorm some collaborative activities based on the student use indicated in the standard.
3. Design a reciprocal teaching activity to replace a unit for which you currently lecture and give individual assignments. If you can, implement the activity and compare student responses to the older method.
4. How do students obtain social information differently than nonsocial information? Do different principles apply to social information compared to nonsocial information?

REFERENCES

Jorczak, Robert L. "An Information Processing Perspective on Divergence and Convergence in Collaborative Learning." *International Journal of Computer-Supported Collaborative Learning* 6, no. 2 (2011): 207–21.

Jorczak, Robert L., and William Bart. "The Effect of Task Characteristics on Conceptual Conflict and Information Processing in Online Discussion." *Computers in Human Behavior* 25, no. 5 (2009): 1165–71.

Kanuka, Heather. "The Influence of Instructional Methods on the Quality of Online Discussion." *The International Review of Research in Open and Distributed Learning* 6, no. 3 (2006).

10

USING THE I-E INSTRUCTIONAL MODEL TO DESIGN HIGH-QUALITY INSTRUCTION

What this chapter is about: This chapter brings together recommendations from the I-E instructional model in a series of steps for creating or improving an instructional design.

Why that matters: It may be difficult for instructors to see how to use principles of the I-E model to achieve a higher-quality instructional design. This chapter surveys the overall procedure of designing instruction based on an instructional model.

The I-E instructional model focuses on supporting student internalization and externalization. Instructors support those processes by presenting information in an easily processed form and having students do activities in which they express their knowledge. Several learning variables mentioned in previous chapters are at the center of efforts to design better information presentation and more effective learning activities. This chapter outlines a procedure for creating new instruction based on evidence-based theory, but existing instruction can be improved by following a similar procedure.

The design procedure generally includes reviewing aspects of learning objectives, specifying information presentation, and identifying learning activities and assessments. By better setting the values of learning variables associated with these tasks in a way that is consistent with the principles of the I-E model, instructors can increase instructional quality.

INSTRUCTIONAL DESIGN STEPS

Units of instruction (modules or lessons) are defined as one or more instructional methods that address one or more learning objectives (outcomes). So learning goals and objectives must be stated prior to designing instruction. Before determining the instructional methods for each module, a *general* instructional plan should specify the overall course or curriculum goals, specify the sequence of units to address all the learning goals, and identify overall course instructional strategies appropriate for the goals, environment, and students. The general design sets boundaries and provides guidance for specification of course modules.

The general plan is determined by the nature of the topic, targeted learning goals, instructional preferences, and logic. The budget and aspects of the instructional delivery environment also contribute to the general design. Identifying overall learning goals is a necessary first of five steps:

1. Identify targeted learning goals for the course.
2. Specify or clarify learning objectives for the goals.
3. Organize course units into a sequence, each addressing one or more objectives.
4. Select overall instructional strategies.
5. Specify instructional methods for each module. This step has a series of substeps discussed below.

Step 1: Identify Course/Curriculum Learning Goals

General course goals are often not determined by the instructor. Business managers, for example, determine what they want trainees to be able to do. School administrators or boards often determine what courses will be offered and what topics the courses address. States provide minimum competency standards for some K–12 subjects. Learning goals can be stated quite generally and need not be explicitly measurable, but they form the basis for more specific and measurable objectives of the course design.

Step 2: Identify and Clarify Target Learning Objectives

Many sources of learning goals, such as the Common Core State Standards (CCSS) or other state standards, specify targeted measurable learning outcomes related to overall goals (i.e., learning objectives or outcomes). Instructors also inherit learning objectives from previous instructors or other sources. Teachers and instructors therefore expect that no writing or further processing of objectives is required. Often, this assumption is incorrect.

As explained previously, high-quality objectives include specification of the *type* and *use* of targeted knowledge. Unfortunately, sources of learning objectives often do not sufficiently specify either the knowledge type or expected use that is required to correctly link instructional methods to learning outcomes.

Instructors often must rewrite and clarify objectives. (A later section of this chapter reviews the analysis and rewriting of instructional objectives to meet minimum requirements in detail.) The outcome of this step is a list of sufficiently specified learning objectives. It is essential for high-quality instruction that proper learning objectives be sufficiently specified.

Step 3: Organize Objectives into a Sequence of Units

The set of learning objectives addressed by the course should be organized into instructional units that each address one objective or a set of closely related objectives. A logical sequence of units is then specified indicating the order in which objectives will be addressed by instruction. The outcome of this step is a road map of instructional units and the learning objectives for each unit. A schedule for student completion of units can then be set for fixed-length instruction.

Step 4: Select Instructional Strategies

Given that the type and use of targeted objectives are adequately specified for each instructional unit, the next task is to determine general instructional strategies that will guide the selection of instructional methods. The general design should provide guidance about preferred instructional strategies for target students.

For example, will the course tend to employ high or low guidance? Will a collaborative or individualistic goal structure be used? What sorts of resources will be considered? What types of online resources are preferred? How will learning be assessed?

These course-wide strategies guide decisions for selecting and designing instructional methods for course units. Evidence-based learning and instructional principles are the basis for selection of appropriate strategies. The nature of targeted students and the instructional delivery environment also provide a basis for putting some design stakes in the ground.

A general design plan should specify which information sources will be the default or primary source for all instructional units (e.g., a textbook). A strategy could specify that information presentation will be mainly asynchronous to accommodate wide variations in student aptitude or because the targeted adult students need to be able to access information when they have the time.

A strategy could also direct that learning activities will be primarily collaborative with minimal instructor guidance. Course designers may decide they have the resources to implement individualized instruction, implying a structure for preassessment of knowledge and instruction that varies in which outcomes are addressed for each student.

Instructional strategies are also influenced by the personal instructional style or philosophy of the instructor. It is entirely possible that specific instructors are better able to implement some strategies than others. However, basing strategies on ill-founded ideology or currently in vogue methods because instructors prefer them is unlikely to be effective.

Strategies should not be so rigid that instructional methods for atypical units cannot vary from the overall plan. Specific methods in units may stray from the specified strategies (with good reasons). Despite such flexibility, strategies should generally narrow the scope of choices for succeeding steps for most instructional units.

Assessment strategy should also be generally determined. For example, which types of assessments will be generally used in the course (e.g., short-answer exams or performance assessments)? This decision is often based mainly on the types of target learning outcomes. Assessment strategy should provide guidance for the type (e.g., summative or formative, traditional versus performance, etc.) and function of assessments (e.g., to determine if prerequisites are met, to assign course grades, etc.).

Other examples of assessment strategy questions include: Will the overall course objectives be assessed in a summative exam? What approach will be used for assessment in each module? What kinds of assessments are preferred (e.g., tests, performance assessments, portfolios, etc.)? What will happen on the basis of assessment? Will students be given grades and will such grades be based more on performance results or student effort and completion of tasks? How frequently will assessments be given?

Analyzing and Rewriting Learning Outcomes

Prior to discussing Step 5, which includes several substeps for designing each unit, analysis and rewriting of learning goals and objectives are discussed in detail via an example. The standard in the example is for science instruction. The CCSS (Common Core State Standards) do not include science standards, so the well-respected standards from the state of Minnesota will be the source of science goals and objectives.

The Minnesota Academic Standards (MAS) for K–12 science (http://education.state.mn.us/MDE/fam/stds/) are organized by grade level and also by four "strands" that are the same for every grade level (the nature of science and engineering, physical science, earth and space science, and life science).

A standard comprises a general description, which can be viewed as an overall statement of the learning goal, and also one or more "benchmarks" that are more specific and measurable objectives. Here is an example of a fifth-grade standard with three benchmarks:

Strand: 5.1 Nature of science and engineering

> Substrand: 5.1.1 The practice of science
> Standard: 5.1.1.1 Understand that science is a way of knowing about the natural world, is done by individuals and groups, and is characterized by empirical criteria, logical argument and skeptical review.
> Benchmark 5.1.1.1.1 Explain why evidence, clear communication, accurate record keeping, replication by others, and openness to scrutiny are essential parts of doing science.
> Benchmark 5.1.1.1.2 Recognize that when scientific investigations are replicated they generally produce the same results, and when results differ significantly, it is important to investigate what may have caused such differences.
> Benchmark 5.1.1.1.3 Understand that different explanations for the same observations usually lead to making more observations and trying to resolve the differences.

From the standard, one might assume that benchmarks would address empirical criteria, logical argument, and skeptical perspective. As written, the benchmarks do not clearly address those concepts. Benchmarks reference new concepts connected to the standard.

Benchmark 1 addresses three concepts: evidence, accurate record keeping, and replication; all concepts related to empirical criteria. Benchmark 2 provides a definition of scientific repetition, which is not explicitly mentioned in the standard (and is only one aspect of scientific investigation). Benchmark 3 is about how differences in theory are resolved (i.e., more observations), which does not seem to be related to any of the three characteristics of science presented in the standard.

A better and more consistent set of benchmarks than those in this MAS standard would address definitions of empirical criteria, logical argument, and skeptical review in more detail. The omission of such benchmarks means, unfortunately, the instructional designer or instructor will have to add them.

As an example of how to rewrite the standard and benchmarks to achieve clarity and better alignment between standard and benchmarks, consider the following rewrites.

> Rewritten Standard 5.1.1.1: Understand that science is a way of knowing that uses empirical criteria, logical argument, and skeptical review.

General and vague terms like "understand" can be used in standards, but actual benchmarks should be as specific as possible in terms of measureable knowledge type and use. Objectives (i.e., benchmarks for MAS) must use specific verbs that can be assessed.

The benchmarks of this standard, as originally written, use three verbs: explain, recognize, and understand. These verbs are different than the use categories of the popular Anderson and Krathwohl (2001) taxonomy or the taxonomy mentioned in chapter 1. Standards writers tend to ignore established taxonomies and use their own, less well-defined terms that make alignment of standards to instructional methods more difficult. Also, the standard includes an additional outcome further complicating alignment ("recall that groups or individuals can do science").

The phrase "explain why" is especially problematic because it can be interpreted as a very high-level use that may be too ambitious for fifth-grade students. Many college students cannot explain why this list of factors is important for scientific method. An alternative use verb is "explain that," which seeks recall of the list of factors of scientific method.

Explaining *why* requires knowledge of principles—the relationship of science practice to its defining characteristics. In contrast, explaining *that* science requires evidence, clear communication, and so on consists of recalling the four defining characteristics of scientific method given in the benchmark. Which type of explaining is intended in this case is up for interpretation by the instructor. A better benchmark could be stated like this:

> B1: Make a paraphrased list of essential parts of doing science that includes clear communication, accurate records, empirical testing, replication of testing, an openness to scrutiny.

"Recognize" (used in the second benchmark) should signify classification, but no classification task seems appropriate for this objective. Are students supposed to recognize when replicated data does not match, or are they expected to know what to do when it does not match? Presumably, a definition of replication is addressed in fourth grade, but we cannot be sure this benchmark is not intended to simply expect students to define experimental replication. The second benchmark could be rewritten like this:

B2: State that replication of scientific investigations is necessary to confirm results and, when results differ, that scientists investigate what may have caused differences.

The verb "understand" in the third benchmark is almost useless for specifying how we expect students to use their knowledge because no observable use of information is specified. Exactly what this benchmark wants the student to be able to do is unclear. Understanding entails too many different behaviors. Should the student be able to identify or recall what should happen if two "explanations" explain a result? Or should the student be able to recall the circumstances under which additional observations are needed? This benchmark would be easier to align to if written like this:

B3: Recognize that when observations are explained by two or more incompatible explanations (theories or hypotheses), additional observations are required to distinguish which explanation is less wrong.

The *type* of knowledge in the benchmarks is also open to interpretation. Is the first benchmark about facts, concepts, or some higher-order procedure that provides valid explanations? The third benchmark seems to be a principle—that increased differences in explanations (i.e., theories and hypotheses) lead scientists to make more observations (i.e., test further hypotheses). Explicit statement of the type of knowledge in a benchmark is required to make higher-quality instructional designs.

This examination of MAS is meant to illustrate that provided learning outcomes may still need instructor processing to translate them into a form that can more directly inform how to apply evidence-based principles in improving instruction. In addition, such standards may be incomplete, and the instructor may have to write more objectives. Provided learning outcomes often require more work by an instructor to determine exactly which type and use of knowledge is targeted.

Step 5: Specify Instructional Methods for Each Module

After specifying the general design, the next step addresses designating instructional methods for each unit specified in the course structure. Step 5 has four substeps for each instructional unit:

1. Select or create assessments.
2. Evaluate potential information and select.
3. Designate or create learning activities.
4. Implement design (deliver instruction).

Substep 5.1: Select or Create Assessments

Once learning objectives are sufficiently specified, course structure is determined, and overall instructional and assessment strategies identified, the next step is to create assessments for each unit. Creation of assessment includes stating what assessments will be given (e.g., pre- and postinstruction summative, instructional quizzes), writing test items, and creating grading rubrics for each unit.

Instructors may find creating assessments prior to specifying instruction difficult. Writing assessments based solely on target learning outcomes often leads to concerns that some targeted learning may be overlooked because instruction has additional objectives. This situation raises the question of why instruction is targeting objectives that are not listed. Instructors may have additional objectives for various reasons, but such objectives should be stated even if such objectives were not included in the overall design.

The omission of objectives from the general design highlights the fact that many common sets of learning standards address "minimum competencies" and are therefore not comprehensive. Educators and standards writers expect that additional learning will occur beyond what is specified. If additional learning is targeted beyond stated standards, such objectives should be explicitly stated in the course design and not simply assumed.

The incomplete nature of standards means that instructors often must write additional standards or edit existing standards. Explicit instructional objectives make possible higher-quality assessment and instructional alignment. If a targeted learning outcome is not important enough to write an objective for, it is not important enough to assess.

For example, recall the rewritten benchmark 3: *Recognize that when observations are explained by two or more explanations (theories), additional observations are required to distinguish which explanation is less wrong.* This is knowledge of a procedure (basically, scientific method) and the use verb is "recognize." Thus an appropriate assessment would provide examples of two or more theories explaining specific results (observations) and have the students select what the appropriate response by scientists would be.

Contrast this item to asking what scientists should do if alternative explanations both explain observations. While this second item is more general, the first better tests application and understanding of the principle rather than just recall of the principle.

The two key points regarding assessment in this model of instructional design are that (1) assessments are best written prior to the design of instructional methods, and (2) standards are unlikely to be sufficiently comprehensive and therefore instructors will likely have to write additional objectives to fully specify instructional goals.

Substep 5.2: Select Information Sources

Information sources are the basis for student internalization of information. Typical information sources include books, lectures, and recorded audio and video. Two characteristics of sources are among the important variables for the selection task: (1) information content in the sources and (2) the medium used to convey information.

Information content is obviously most important. An important design task is to ascertain whether a potential information source provides relevant and adequate information to support internalization to meet learning objectives. Of secondary interest is how information is presented—which often involves the characteristics of the information storage and transmission medium (see the chapter on variables of information presentation).

Content of Information Sources Instructional designers want to present information that is relevant to the target learning objectives and appropriate to the information-receiving abilities of target students. Information relevance is determined by whether information supports internalization of knowledge related to performance of the target objectives.

Simply providing a source of information, however, may not be sufficient. If a textbook is selected for a course, then appropriate readings within the book must be identified. Merely assigning students to read chapters likely has them cover information irrelevant to targeted learning. Higher-quality selection of information must have students read specific pages and passages that are relevant to targeted learning or must provide information sources that only address targeted learning objectives.

Instructors can designate their own lectures or lecture-discussion as information sources. This selection has the advantage that the instructor can tailor the information to objectives and students. The downside is that instructors must devote considerable time and effort to creating and delivering the information relative to designating existing sources.

Presentation Characteristics of Information Sources Beyond selection of information, the medium and learner control capabilities of sources should be considered. The I-E model identifies learning variables of presentation, such as reviewability and self-pacing. Such selection will depend on the nature of the information, type of learning objective, instructional delivery environment, and characteristics of students.

Typically, instruction references printed materials (e.g., a textbook), which are read asynchronously by students. Printed sources present text and image information that is self-paced and reviewable. Text requires reading skills that vary greatly among grade levels but also among students within a grade level. Online recorded audio or audio video lectures are asynchronous and reviewable.

For example, consider the rewritten benchmark 3: *Recognize that when observations are explained by two or more explanations (theories), additional observations are required to distinguish which explanation is less wrong.* An instructional designer could look for information that states this principle and also includes information in the form of examples of how different explanations can explain similar observational results. The examples should include information about how scientists react by making more observation in the hope of finding which explanation is scientifically superior.

Substep 5.3: Select Learning Activities

For each unit, instructional designers must designate (select or create) learning activities that have students externalize their knowledge in ways that promote new or improved knowledge related to learning objectives. This task is guided by principles relating learning variables to externalization. Despite lack of a good theoretical model of learning by externalization, advice about the effectiveness of learning activities is easy to find. Such advice is, however, often based on best practices or ideology rather than evidence or empirically supported learning theory.

The main recommendation from the I-E model is that the *use* specified in target learning objectives suggests what students should do in a learning activity. Characteristics of students and the environment also should guide selection of learning activities. Some types of activities cannot be implemented online, and some are much easier and less expensive to implement for specific instructional environments.

Taking quizzes and doing drills are traditional externalizations that have evidence of supporting some types of learning. Writing papers, making concept maps, giving presentations, and constructing products are all examples of types of externalizations. Some activities combine presentation of new information with externalization, such as interactive computer-delivered tutorials or peer discussion.

To support benchmark 3 as rewritten above, an instructional designer might choose an activity in which an observation is explained by different theories or hypotheses and have the student suggest how the situation should be addressed from a scientific perspective (or this could be part of a lab activity). Feedback would specify that making more observations could distinguish which theory is correct. Effectiveness of this activity likely is unaffected by synchronicity, high learner control, or type of mediation, though examples related to a student's lab results provide greater authenticity.

The outcome of this substep is a designated learning activity (or set of activities) for each unit. The designation of assessments, information resources, and learning activities complete the specification of the instructional methods used for each unit. All that remains is to implement the design for each module.

Substep 5.4: Implement Design (Schedule, Feedback, Grading, etc.)

While this chapter focuses on design of instruction, design is not the whole story. Instructors implement a design by scheduling time for instruction to address objectives, directing students to information sources, and explaining how to do learning activities and assessments. So instructors must prepare written documents or orally provide instructions that inform students about what to do within a course unit.

In addition, instructors can present information via classroom lectures or recorded online lectures. To accomplish these tasks, instructors must decide what they are going to say and then deliver the lecture in real time or record the lecture and provide students access to the recording. Instructors also often elaborate and clarify information presented in other sources.

In classrooms, instructors and students are present so the instructor can synchronously monitor student activity and provide clarification and redirection as necessary to keep students on track. In online courses, instructors must produce more guidance via written material to better explain how students should proceed within an instructional unit. Online instructors can receive asynchronous messages requesting clarification and should make that process understood and easy. Online instruction requires that instructors present more written reminders about what student actions are pending because students do not meet in regular classes in which they are reminded by the instructor or other students about what is due or what to do next.

During delivery of instruction, instructors also must evaluate student externalizations and provide feedback about them. Instructors online must write text feedback (or record audio) using options provided by the learning management system that provides online functions. Methods using asynchronous peer discussion require instructors to monitor discussion and write feedback to keep students on track for productive discussion.

It should be understood that implementing an instructional design leaves ample room for variation based on the characteristics of individual instructors. The instruction of two instructors will vary even if they are following the same design. A better-specified design, however, has a better chance of resulting in better instruction despite instructor differences. Instructors that are aware of evidence-based instructional principles will deliver better-quality instruction regardless of the quality of the design.

INSTRUCTIONAL METHODS FOR ELEMENTARY GRADE LEVELS

While early grades also use mediated sources of information, including workbooks and videos, typical instructional methods used in elementary classrooms rely on oral presentation of information by the instructor.

Such presentation methods are better for the youngest students because they are poor readers. Face-to-face interaction is how children first learn and is most comfortable for most students (even in later grades).

Even very young students tend to have a schema for stories (i.e., a story grammar) and so stories are often used to present information verbally. Humans, in general, better understand stories because all were taught to read using stories. Narrative text such as found in textbooks do not use stories and thus a story grammar does not help students understand such books. (This fact has caused most textbooks to include a story at the beginning of each chapter.) Whether information is presented in a story is another variable for instructional designers to consider.

Conceptual conflict may not be as important for younger students, who do not have as many consolidated concepts and beliefs as older students. Elementary students are known to generally like school and display a strong motivation to learn, which lessens the need for making information and assignments interesting based on individual student differences. Cultural differences, however, may be important in maintaining young student interest and understanding because they may have limited contact with the dominant culture.

Learning activities in the early grades tend to be done synchronously in class with high teacher oral guidance and feedback. Younger students are presumed to require more instructional guidance. Practice for obtaining and consolidating skills is an important activity, so drill and practice in which students are given multiple tasks and/or questions with feedback is an important learning activity for young students.

SUMMARY FOR INSTRUCTIONAL DESIGN PROCEDURE

An instructional design is a plan for instruction. Higher-quality instruction results from a plan that follows learning and instruction principles that specify learning variables. An instructional design specifies how learning variables will be set for a course to meet the goals of instruction. A general design states learning goals and objectives of instruction and organizes objectives into instructional units. The general design also sets instructional strategies based on learning and instructional principles, preferably from an empirically validated learning theory such as information processing learning theory.

Each instructional unit addresses one or more objectives. A more detailed design specifies assessments, information resources, and learning activities for each instructional unit. Unit components are selected based on principles matching learning variables to learning outcomes for specific types of students.

Learning variables for information selection include relevance, appropriateness, interest for students, and conceptual conflict. Variables of information presentation include the amount and organization of presented information, the sensory mode and medium, degree of learner control, and synchronicity. The selection of learning activities is based on learning variables including student prior knowledge, type of targeted learning outcomes, authenticity, feedback, instructor guidance, and conceptual conflict.

Considering these variables, and choosing unit components based on how they set these variables, will result in higher instructional quality and better student achievement. Effort extended to design based on evidence-based principles will pay dividends including more efficient and effective instruction.

QUESTIONS

1. Review a set of learning standards relevant to what you teach. Analyze them especially in regard to type of knowledge and student use.
2. Rewrite at least one goal and objective that is currently used in your instruction.
3. For a unit that you typically teach (or will teach), describe how information resources were selected. Critique those resources based on learning variables that may affect instructional effectiveness.
4. For a unit that you typically teach (or will teach), describe how learning activities were selected. Characterize those activities in terms of how students must use their knowledge to do the activity.

BIBLIOGRAPHY

Anderson, Lorin W., and David R. Krathwohl. *A Taxonomy for Learning, Teaching, and Assessing: A Revision of Bloom's Taxonomy of Educational Objectives*. New York: Longman, 2001.

Atkinson, R. C., and R. M. Shiffrin. "Human Memory: A Proposed System and Its Control Processes." In *The Psychology of Learning and Motivation: Advances in Research and Theory Vol. 2*, edited by K. W. Spence and J. T. Spence, 89–195. New York: Academic Press, 1968.

Boruch, R., D. DeMoya, and B. Snyder. "The Importance of Randomized Field Trials in Education and Related Areas." In *Evidence Matters: Randomized Trials in Education Research*, edited by F. Mosteller and R. Boruch, 50–79. Washington, DC: Brookings Institution Press, 2002.

Brophy, Jere E., and Thomas L. Good. "Teacher Behavior and Student Achievement." In *Handbook of Research on Teaching*, edited by M. C. Wittrock, 328–75. New York: Macmillan, 1986.

Carroll, John B. "The Carroll Model: A 25-Year Retrospective and Prospective View." *Educational Researcher* 18, no. 1 (1989): 26.

Clark, Richard E. "Media Will Never Influence Learning." *Educational Technology Research and Development* 42, no. 2 (1994): 21–29.

Craik, Fergus I., and Endel Tulving. "Depth of Processing and the Retention of Words in Episodic Memory." *Journal of Experimental Psychology: General* 104, no. 3 (1975): 268–94.

Craik, Fergus I. M., and Robert S. Lockhart. "Levels of Processing: A Framework for Memory Research." *Journal of Verbal Learning and Verbal Behavior* 11.6 (1972) 671–84.

Johnson, Scott D., and Jenny Daugherty. "Quality and Characteristics of Recent Research in Technology Education." *Journal of Technology Education* 20.1 (2008): 16–31.

Jorczak, Robert L. "An Information Processing Perspective on Divergence and Convergence in Collaborative Learning." *International Journal of Computer-Supported Collaborative Learning* 6, no. 2 (2011): 207–21.

Jorczak, Robert L., and William Bart. "The Effect of Task Characteristics on Conceptual Conflict and Information Processing in Online Discussion." *Computers in Human Behavior* 25, no. 5 (2009): 1165–71.

Kanuka, Heather. "The Influence of Instructional Methods on the Quality of Online Discussion." *The International Review of Research in Open and Distributed Learning* 6, no. 3 (2006).

Karpicke, Jeffery. D. "Retrieval-Based Learning: Active Retrieval Promotes Meaningful Learning." *Current Directions in Psychological Science* 21, no. 3 (2012): 157–63.

Mayer, R. E., and R. Moreno. "A Cognitive Theory of Multimedia Learning: Implications for Design Principles." 1998. http://www.unm.edu/~moreno/PDFS/chi.pdf.

Mayer, Richard E. *Multimedia Learning*. Cambridge: Cambridge University Press, 2001.

Means, B., Y. Toyama, R. Murphy, M. Bakia, and K. Jones. *Evaluation of Evidence Based Practices in Online Learning: A Meta Analysis and Review of Online Learning Studies*. Washington, DC: U.S. Department of Education Office of Planning Evaluation and Policy Development, 2009.

Morris, C. D., J. D Bransford, and J. J. Franks. "Levels of Processing Versus Transfer-Appropriate Processing." *Journal of Verbal Learning and Verbal Behavior* 16 (1977): 519–33.

Pashler, Harold, Mark McDaniel, Doug Rohrer, and Robert Bjork. "Learning Styles: Concepts and Evidence." *Psychological Science in the Public Interest* 9, no. 3 (2009): 105–19.

Phye, Gary D. *Handbook of Classroom Assessment: Learning, Achievement, and Adjustment*. San Diego: Academic Press, 1997.

Pinker, Steven. *How the Mind Works*. New York: Norton, 1997.

Roediger, Henry L., and Jeffrey D. Karpicke. "The Power of Testing Memory." *Perspectives on Psychological Science* 1, no. 3 (Sept. 2006): 181–210.

Rosenshine, B., and R. Stevens. "Teaching Functions." In *Handbook of Research on Teaching*, edited by M. C. Wittrock, 376–91. New York: MacMillan, 1986.

Schochet, Peter Z., and Hanley S. Chiang. "Error Rates in Measuring Teacher and School Performance Based on Student Test Score Gains" (NCEE 2010–4004). Washington, DC: National Center for Education Evaluation and Regional Assistance, Institute of Education Sciences, U.S. Department of Education (2010).

Soar, Robert S. *An Integrative Approach to Classroom Learning*. Philadelphia: Temple University, 1966.

Soar, Robert S. and Soar, R. M. "An Empirical Analysis of Selected Follow-Through Programs: An Example of a Process Approach to Evaluation." In *Early Childhood Education*, edited by I. J. Gordon, 229–59. Chicago: National Society for the Study of Education, 1972.

Squire, Larry R. "Memory Systems of the Brain: A Brief History and Current Perspective." *Neurobiology of Learning and Memory* 82, no. 3 (2004): 171–77.

Sweller, John. "Cognitive Load during Problem Solving: Effects on Learning." *Cognitive Science* 12, no. 2 (1988): 257–85.

Sweller, John, and Graham A. Cooper. "The Use of Worked Examples as a Substitute for Problem Solving in Learning Algebra." *Cognition and Instruction* 2, no. 1 (1985): 59–89.

Tulving, Endel, and Donald M. Thomson. "Encoding Specificity and Retrieval Processes in Episodic Memory." *Psychological Review* 80, no. 5 (1973): 352–73.

U.S. Department of Education. *Non-regulatory Guidance: Using Evidence to Strengthen Educational Investments*. Washington, DC: Department of Education, 2016.

INDEX

active learning, 25, 32, 78, 91
aptitude-treatment interaction, 74
assessment, 92; strategy, 119; creation, 123
asyncronicity, 73; in design, 118; in learning activities, 99; in media, 77, 110; in MOOCs, 101; online messages, 127
ATI. *See* aptitude treatment interaction
attention, 47, 74; and active learning, 25; Carroll's perseverance, 60; conscious, 48; and relevance, 67; and student interest, 67

blended instruction environment. *See* hybrid instructional environment
Bloom's taxonomy of learning, 6

Carroll Model of School Learning, 58
cognitive control processes, 46
cognitive load, 42; extraneous, 70; and redundancy, 71; theory, 61
Coleman Report, 3
conceptual change, 7; and conceptual conflict, 90; information selection for, 69; and semantic knowledge, 45
conceptual conflict, 68; in collaborative learning, 106; for conceptual change, 69; for discussion tasks, 108; as externalization variable, 90; as presentation variable, 68; principle, 91;
for young students, 128
consolidation, 42, 46
constructivism, 28
control process. *See* cognitive control processes
correlational study. *See* descriptive study
coverage, 70

declarative memories, 43
descriptive study, 14
differentiated instruction, 4, 75

educational technology, 30, 70, 77
elaboration, 70, 83
Elaboration Theory, 56, 70
elaborative rehearsal, 48, 65
encoding, 40, 46; and meaning, 44
encoding specificity principle, 50
environmental learning variable, 60, 62, 67
evidence, 11, 12
evidence-based research, 11; as a buzzword, 16
executive functions, 49
experiment, 13, 15
explicit memory, 43

feedback, 88, 92, 127; principle, 89; types, 89
flipped instruction, 99

Gagne's Conditions of Learning, 56, 65
generative outcomes, 7

higher-order: knowledge, 27, 45; outcomes/learning, 49, 85, 93
hybrid instructional environments, 99
hypertext, 70
hypothesis, 11

IES. *See* Institute of Education Sciences
ILPT. *See* information processing learning theory
implicit knowledge/memory, 43, 46
incidental learning, 47
individualized instruction, 4, 31, 59, 75, 101, 118
information processing learning theory (ILPT), 35, 40, 57
Institute of Education Sciences (IES), 16
instructional design, ix, 56, 85, 127; steps, 116
instructional guidance, 89; as constructivist principle, 28; and younger students, 128
instructional improvement, 3, 22
instructional method, 57, 91, 93, 101
instructional strategy, 56; collaborative, 97; select, 118
instructional theory/model, 56
intentional learning, 47
intermediate (term) memory, 40, 42
internalization, 50, 65
intervention, educational, 17

learner control, 28, 89; of computer-based instruction, 77; of presentation, 72; of testing, 94
learning activity/assignment/task, 85, 126; and assessment, 92; and higher-order outcomes, 87; student selection, 90
learning hierarchy, 56
learning management system (LMS), 31, 127
learning objectives/outcomes, 3, 6, 81; identifying and clarifying, 117; rewriting, 119; for selecting learning activities, 126
learning styles, 24

learning theory, 36; Cognitive Load Theory (CLT), 61; and instructional theory, 55; Multimedia Learning Theory (MMLT), 61
learning variable, 58, 66
lecturing, lectures, 25, 72, 76; and flipping, 100
levels-of-processing principle, 49, 86
LMS. *See* learning management system

maintenance rehearsal, 48, 65
meaningful learning, 44
medium (information), 72, 110, 124; digital media, 93
meta analysis, 17
metacognition, 6, 32, 38
modal memory model, 40
MOOC (massive open online courses), 101
multimedia, 77; principle, 72
Multimedia Learning Theory (MMLT), 61, 70
multi-tiered system of support (MTSS), 59, 101

non-declarative memory, 43

Piaget, Jean, 38
procedural memory, 44, 107

quasi-experiment, 14

rehearsal cognitive process, 38
Reigeluth, Charles. *See* Elaboration Theory
retrieval, 47

schema, 44, 48, 60, 69, 71, 83, 88
scientific principle, 35
scientific theory, 36
self-assessment, 94
semantic memories/knowledge, 43, 45, 47; learning for, 48
semantic network, 44
sensory store, 41
short-term memory (STM), 41, 59
social development theory, 38
standardized (high stakes) tests, 93
story grammar, 128

structured academic controversy (SAC), 109
student-centered learning, 77
student learning variables, 59
synchronicity: of information presentation, 73, 74; and medium of discussion, 110; of online versus classroom, 99
synchronous learning activities in classroom/online, 99, 100

taxonomy, learning outcomes, 6, 7, 121; higher-order outcomes, 45

teacher-centered learning, 78, 111
testing for learning, 93, 94
textbooks, 57, 72, 76, 124, 128
transfer appropriate processing, 49, 86
21st Century Learning Outcomes, 27

Vygotsky, Lev, 38, 82, 106

working memory, 41, 46, 65, 70, 83; and cognitive load, 61; and multimedia principle, 62
working memory capacity, 41, 59

ABOUT THE AUTHOR

Dr. Robert Jorczak is an educational psychologist and researcher who has taught every educational level from kindergarten to graduate school. He has been an instructional designer and educational technology consultant for corporate and academic clients for more than twenty years. Dr. Jorczak has earned an MA and PhD in educational psychology from the University of Minnesota, Twin Cities, in addition to an MS in computer science and a BA in education from the University of Illinois at Urbana-Champaign.

www.ingramcontent.com/pod-product-compliance
Lightning Source LLC
Chambersburg PA
CBHW020742230426
43665CB00009B/526